MODERN POLITICAL ANALYSIS

FOURTH EDITION

Robert A. Dahl
Yale University

Prentice-Hall, Inc., Englewood Cliffs, New Jersey 07632

Library of Congress Cataloging in Publication Data

Dahl, Robert Alan, (date)
Modern political analysis.

(Prentice-Hall foundations of modern political science series)
Includes index.
1. Power (Social sciences) 2. Political science.
I. Title. II. Series.
JC330.D34 1983 320 83-3288
ISBN 0-13-596973-5
ISBN 0-13-596965-4 (pbk.)

PRENTICE-HALL FOUNDATIONS OF MODERN POLITICAL SCIENCE SERIES

Robert A. Dahl, Editor

Printed in the United States of America

10 9 8 7 6 5 4 3 2 1

Editorial/production supervision and
interior design: Virginia Cavanagh Neri
Cover design: Wanda Lubelska Design/Beata Petek, Designer
Manufacturing buyer: Ron Chapman

ISBN 0-13-596973-5
ISBN 0-13-596965-4 {pbk.}

Prentice-Hall International, Inc., *London*
Prentice-Hall of Australia Pty. Limited, *Sydney*
Editora Prentice-Hall do Brasil, Ltda., *Rio de Janeiro*
Prentice-Hall Canada Inc., *Toronto*
Prentice-Hall of India Private Limited, *New Delhi*
Prentice-Hall of Japan, Inc., *Tokyo*
Prentice-Hall of Southeast Asia Pte. Ltd., *Singapore*
Whitehall Books Limited, *Wellington, New Zealand*

MODERN POLITICAL ANALYSIS

PRENTICE-HALL FOUNDATIONS OF MODERN POLITICAL SCIENCE SERIES

Robert A. Dahl, Editor

THE AGE OF IDEOLOGY-POLITICAL THOUGHT, 1750 TO THE PRESENT, Second Edition
by Isaac Kramnick and Frederick M. Watkins

THE AMERICAN PARTY SYSTEM AND THE AMERICAN PEOPLE, Second Edition
by Fred I. Greenstein

THE ANALYSIS OF INTERNATIONAL RELATIONS, Second Edition
by Karl W. Deutsch

CONGRESS AND THE PRESIDENCY, Third Edition
by Nelson W. Polsby

DATA ANALYSIS FOR POLITICS AND POLICY
by Edward R. Tufte

MODERN POLITICAL ANALYSIS, Fourth Edition
by Robert A. Dahl

MODERN POLITICAL ECONOMY
by Norman Frohlich and Joe A. Oppenheimer

THE POLICY-MAKING PROCESS, Second Edition
by Charles E. Lindblom

PUBLIC ADMINISTRATION
by James W. Fesler

CONTENTS

PREFACE

This edition reflects a recent, important, and, I hope, enduring change—the revival of Anglo-American political philosophy, or normative political theory. When the first edition appeared in 1963, the most rapid and, I believe, most significant developments were taking place in empirical political analysis. Empirical work has continued to flourish.

Meanwhile, still another change has contributed to the growth and health of empirical analysis: the increasing universality of political science. It is no great exaggeration to say that in 1963 political science as a special field of scholarship and university teaching was, with only a few important exceptions, mainly confined to the United States. Elsewhere, for the most part, the study of politics was still a servant to law, history, or philosophy. Thus either little systematic empirical analysis of political life took place in most other countries, or if it did, it was predominantly legal, historical, or philosophical—or else it was undertaken by Americans. In spite of the best intentions and training, the danger was that empirical political analysis would become somewhat parochial because of the influence of American experiences and intellectual trends. During the last two decades, however, political science has expanded rapidly in many other countries, to the long-run benefit, I believe, of the field.

However, for reasons discussed in Chapter 9 of this edition, political philosophy with its particular emphasis on fundamental questions of value was, by comparison, lacking in creativity. But the publication in 1971 of John Rawls's *A Theory of Justice*—however one may judge its validity—unquestionably marks the onset of a period of phenomenal growth of new works in political philosophy, at least in English-speaking countries. Although I called attention to this important development in the previous edition, its magnitude was still unclear. For this edition, I have written a new chapter (Chapter 9) that describes both the decline and the recent revival of political philosophy, and I have used *A Theory of Justice* as a convenient vantage point from which to survey what has been taking place.

For their help in the preparation of this edition, I want to thank Rosita Thomas, who brought much of the cross-national data in the text and in tables up to date. Her research was greatly facilitated by her access to data for the forthcoming work by Charles Lewis Taylor and David A. Jodice, *World Handbook of Political and Social Indicators, Third Edition, Vol. 1: Cross National Attributes and Rates of Change and Vol. 2: Political Protest and Government Change*, to be published in 1983 (New Haven: Yale University Press). I wish to express my great appreciation to Charles Taylor and David A. Jodice for their generosity in permitting me to use their data prior to the publication of their book. I would also like to thank those who read the manuscript for this edition and offered comments, particularly on Chapter 9: James S. Fishkin, Yale University; J. Patrick Dobel, University of Michigan; Sidney A. Pearson, Jr., Radford University; Patrick Riley, University of Wisconsin; and Roz J. Wolff for her sensitive and skillful editing.

Robert A. Dahl

FROM THE PREFACE TO THE THIRD EDITION

As you may have discovered, there are enthusiasts who appear to believe that most (if not all) important knowledge about politics can be found between the covers of a single book—or at least in the works of one author. If one studies my man X deeply enough, an enthusiast will say, one will find that he tells everything. The enthusiast's oracle most likely is some great name—Plato, Aristotle, Machiavelli, or Marx. But the oracle might turn out to be an ex-sportswriter, turned political pundit. I am reasonably sure that the search for a political oracle is in vain. For, I believe, it is a melancholy fact that no one has ever been wise enough to contribute more than a small fraction of what is known about politics.

Our enthusiast has a first cousin who insists that everything important has already been said in the great works of the past, as if wisdom, like wine, must be aged to make it better. Yet one may search long and hard in the great works and not, I am quite sure, find as much about the operation of modern political parties, the American Congress, the political system of the USSR, or a great number of other topics, as one will find in recent studies.

For political institutions change. Modern democracy simply is not equivalent to the Athenian political system or the Roman Republic. Also, the study of politics to some extent is cumulative. Indeed, on certain topics, knowledge increases almost annually. If someone were to ask, "How can I learn about what sorts of people participate most in politics, and why?" I would urge him or her to start with the most recent studies in the field and work back. I seriously doubt that one would get much help from Aristotle, Rousseau, or the *Federalist Papers*.

Yet, I feel it is equally arrogant to suppose that very little worth knowing is to be found outside the more recent works. Recent studies often help us to gain a better judgment on questions of fact—and anyone who is contemptuous of fact had better forget about studying politics. Twenty-five centuries of dedicated study of politics naturally have produced many highly plausible but, unfortunately, contradictory hypotheses. Each can be strongly supported by common sense and can be argued till Doomsday as long as one sticks to the older methods of analysis. Happily, new methods of inquiry and analysis sometimes help us to settle these questions. Yet not all the questions do get answered, and they probably never will. The best of the profound works of the past, even of the distant past, make us aware of what these unanswered questions are. And they present us with the best fruits of creative minds struggling to arrive at answers. We do not know so much today that we can afford to neglect this older wisdom.

Now what, you ask, have these observations to do with a book on modern political analysis? This: Like the series of which it is a part, this book does not pretend to tell you all that you need to know about politics. Its aim is more modest but more realistic: to equip you with a few basic concepts, ideas, and analytical tools—ancient or recent, whichever seem better—so you can proceed more competently toward what should be, in a democracy, a life-long vocation: the analysis of politics.

Robert A. Dahl

MODERN POLITICAL ANALYSIS

1

POLITICAL ANALYSIS: WHY? HOW? WHAT?

WHY ANALYZE POLITICS?

Whether a person likes it or not, virtually no one is completely beyond the reach of some kind of political system. A citizen encounters politics in the government of a country, town, school, church, business firm, trade union, club, political party, civic association, and a host of other organizations. Politics is an unavoidable fact of human existence. Everyone is involved in some fashion at some time in some kind of political system.

If politics is inescapable, so are the consequences of politics. That statement might once have been shrugged off as rhetorical, but today it is a brutal and palpable fact. For whether humankind will be blown to smithereens or will design political arrangements that enable our species to survive is now being determined—by politics and politicians.

The answer to the question, "Why analyze politics?" is, obvious then. We cannot really escape politics—though we may try to ignore it. That is a powerful reason for trying to understand it. You may want to understand politics simply in order to satisfy your curiosity, or to feel that you comprehend what is going on around you, or in order to make the best possible choices among the alternatives open to you—that is, in order to act wisely. Although, for most people, making better choices probably provides the strongest incentive for political analysis, human begins also tend to feel a powerful need to make sense out of their world. To be sure, anyone can make *some* sense out of politics; but politics is an exceptionally complex matter, quite likely one of the most complex matters human beings encounter. The danger is that without skill in dealing with its complexities, one will drastically oversimplify politics. It is fair to say, I think, that most people do oversimplify. Of course, because some simplification is unavoidable, this book also simplifies political complexities; but it does not, I believe, do so excessively. As we shall see, trying to acquire the elementary skills necessary for understanding politics is not a simple task.

HOW

At this point you might ask: If I want to understand politics, why shouldn't I plunge directly into political life and acquire the knowledge I need from direct experience? Doesn't political experience provide better knowledge about politics than books, analysis, theory, and abstractions? Since there is much to be said for knowledge gained from experience, perhaps an analogy will help to show its limits.

From ancient times, the skill of the statesman has been likened to that of the physician: the statesman cares for the political well being of the community, the physician for the health of the people in it. However, modern medicine distinguishes between the practice of medicine—what medical people often call "clinical" medicine—and research into the manifestations, causes, and treatment of disease—the "science" of medicine. Medical practitioners and scientists agree that treating patients requires the special skills of the practitioner, and that in acquiring those skills there is no substitute for direct experience. In premedical and medical training, in the classroom and the laboratory, the mind of the budding practitioner is stuffed full of scientific knowledge. Essential as this knowledge is, however, it is nonetheless inadequate for treating patients. Even after four years of academic training and some clinical exposure, newly minted medical graduates are still too unskilled to be fully entrusted with the treatment of patients. Further medical training therefore demands internship, and in fields of specialization, an additional period of clinical experience, nowadays typically a residency of three or four years. In ways not at all well understood, some physicians acquire an unusual capacity to make wise decisions about the treatment of sick people and may become known to their peers as excellent, even brilliant, clinicians.

Essential as the skills of the practitioner are in treating patients, however, the progress of medicine depends mainly not on the experience of practitioners but on the work of scientists. Many medical scientists have little to do with patients; some might even be inept practitioners. Only in rare cases, it seems, are both kinds of skills developed in the same person. Yet knowledge gained from direct experience with patients, valuable as it is, does not ordinarily lead to new discoveries in medicine: The Nobel prizes go to the great medical scientists, not the great practitioners. Without the work of medical scientists, then, the practitioner could acquire only a feeble understanding—little better than that of doctors in the eighteenth century—of the causes and treatment of diseases. The wise judgment of even the greatest practitioner is only in part—perhaps in small part—a product of direct experience. It is also a product of knowledge gained from generations of scientific research.

Although the analogy ought not to be pushed too far, a similar distinction might be made about ways of acquiring political knowledge. Experience in politics unquestionably provides knowledge that cannot be acquired in any other way. I have found that students who participate in political campaigns or work a stint for a member of Congress or of a state legislature are usually convinced that they have gained knowledge that is different from what they can learn from books and classrooms. They are right in thinking so. Yet, as in medicine, what one can learn from direct experience is necessarily very limited. For example, how could you learn only from your own direct experience what features of a country—El Salvador, let us say—make democracy there likely or unlikely? Or what policies of the United States, if any, would increase or reduce El Salvador's prospects for democracy? Because direct experience is inadequate, political practitioners, like medical practitioners, depend greatly on specialists, including academic specialists. Far more than may be commonly understood, political leaders today are required to make practical judgments about essentially abstract or theoretical questions.

Just as in medicine, however, we must not mistake skill in systematic political analysis with skill in political practice, even though these skills overlap. As in the arts, an analyst, or critic, is not necessarily a gifted performer.

Skill in analyzing politics is not the same as skill in practicing politics. James Madison's speeches at the Constitutional Convention and his chapters in *The Federalist* demonstrate that he was a brilliant political analyst, yet he was a mediocre President. By contrast, Franklin Roosevelt had enormous skill, insight, and astuteness as a political leader and President; yet one cannot find in Roosevelt's messages, state papers, and letters an analysis of how he himself operated as President that seems as valid as the analysis contained in several later studies by scholars. Even if Roosevelt had tried to explain how he operated, could he have succeeded? Skilled artists are frequently unable to explain why or how they do what they do so superbly.

Sometimes, to be sure, skill in political practice does go hand-in-hand with skill in political analysis. Woodrow Wilson was a historian and political scientist before he was a politician. *Congressional Government*, which he wrote in 1884 at the age of twenty-eight, is still worth reading a century later. As governor of New Jersey and as President, Wilson also displayed a high order of skill as a political practitioner—until opposition to his goals during his second term brought out aspects of his personality that severely impaired his skills as a politician.[1] Moreover, all skilled political practitioners must have some capacity for political analysis, even though they may be unable to explain what they know. The rapidly increasing complexity of modern national and international politics requires a corresponding increase in the analytical competence of political leaders. Old fashioned wardheelers whose political knowledge was narrow and parochial were once an effective force in American politics; yet they have all but disappeared because the complexities of an age of highspeed computer technology, nuclear energy, and artificial satellites made them obsolete.

What is true for political leaders is also true for ordinary citizens. In making judgments about political leaders and their policies, understanding and choosing among alternatives, and making sense out of the world's confusing complexities, everyone needs more than direct experience. The aim of political analysis, therefore, is to go beyond what anyone can hope to learn from direct experience.

FOUR ORIENTATIONS

To understand and to act intelligently, we often ask a basic question that will of course vary from one situation to another. The question frequently goes something like this: How can I act in order to arrive at a better state of affairs (for me, my family, my business, my party, my country, the weak and suffering, the strong and able, the people, all of humanity, and so on)? But another question must be asked to answer the first: What would a better state of affairs be? More generally, what distinguishes the better from the worse? However, still a third question must be asked: How do things come about in the real world? For instance, if I believe that peace is better than war, and if I wish to prevent wars, I must therefore do something about the causes of wars. But what *are* the causes of wars? All three questions presuppose answers to a fourth, a question so fundamental that one often takes the answer for granted and is quite unaware that there *is* such a question: What do I *mean* by the key

[1] In his analysis of Wilson's personality and political conduct, Alexander L. George shows that when Wilson met genuinely threatening opposition, as he did during his second term, he "was unable to function expediently and proved singularly gauche as a politician. . . . Wilson became rigidly stubborn and tried to force through his proposal without compromising it." See "Power as a Compensatory Value for Political Leaders," *Journal of Social Issues* 24 (July 1968): 42. See also Alexander L. George and Juliette L. George, *Woodrow Wilson and Colonel House: A Personality Study* (New York: Dover Press, 1964)).

terms I use or the statements I make? For example, how do I define democracy? How do I distinguish it from other forms of government?

Each question represents a different orientation toward the world. In asking the first question, one is oriented to discovering a *policy*. In asking the second, one seeks to discover *norms*, values or criteria, to judge alternative policies. In asking the third question, one seeks to discover *empirical* relationships among elements in the real world. In asking the fourth, one tries to clarify *meaning*. Hence we can speak of a policy orientation, a normative orientation, an empirical orientation, and a semantic orientation. Depending on which question is the focus of attention at any given moment in political analysis, one can speak of policy analysis, normative analysis, empirical analysis, and analysis of meaning (sometimes referred to as conceptual or semantic analysis).

In actual political analysis, however, the boundaries are usually not sharply defined. Moreover, although the four orientations suggest a certain logical relation—choosing a policy presupposes some standards of evaluation, which in turn presuppose some empirical beliefs, which make sense only if the key terms have meaning—political analysis rarely if ever proceeds exactly in this fashion. As we shall see in a moment, while the plan of this book does presuppose the relations that I have just described, it seems to me easier to approach the questions in the reverse order: We shall begin by clarifying the meaning of some of the key terms used in political analysis, move on to some fundamental empirical questions, then proceed to normative analysis, and finally examine the problem of choosing policies.

Before saying more about the plan of the book, however, it will be helpful if we confront a question directed particularly to empirical analysis.

A Query About Empirical Political Analysis: Art or Science?

Is empirical political analysis a science?[2] Or is it an art? I believe it is both. To the extent that many aspects of political analysis are most easily acquired by

[2] American scholars who helped inaugurate the first departments of political science in this country were strongly influenced by scholarship in nineteenth-century Germany, where the term *wissenschaft* connoted not only science but also learning, knowledge, scholarship, and more generally, the intellectual product of any systematic inquiry. Thus the word "science" in "political science" was probably intended to mean something like "systematic study" and not, as it is more likely to be interpreted today, "empirical inquiry in the manner of the natural sciences." For a brief history, see Dwight Waldo, "Political Science: Tradition, Discipline, Profession, Science, Enterprise," in *The Handbook of Political Science*, vol. 1, (Reading, Mass.: Addison-Wesley Publishing Co., Inc., 1975).

In some countries, such as France and Italy, the term political science has been used to cover a number of specialized fields such as law, economics, and sociology. In these countries, political analysis was until recently assumed to be an aspect of each of these fields, but not an autonomous intellectual discipline. Consequently, among the "political sciences" there was no separate field of political science.

practice and training under the supervision of a person already skilled in this area, it is an art. Whenever students of politics scrupulously test their generalizations and theories against the data of experience by means of meticulous observation, classification, and measurement, then empirical political analysis is scientific in its approach. To the extent that this approach actually yields tested propositions of considerable generality, political analysis can be regarded as scientific in its results.

The extent to which empirical political analysis should be approached as an art or a science is a hotly debated issue. And if it is considered a science, there are important differences between those who seek to emulate the natural sciences like physics and chemistry, and those who believe that the study of human beings is inherently different from the study of nature in its nonhuman manifestations.

Many who hold the second view argue that we cannot really understand a human action unless we can grasp its subjective meaning: what it means to the person who performs it, what that person intended by it, and so on. An atomic particle does not intend anything; what it does has no subjective meaning to the physicist. Physics does well as a science by describing activity in purely external, physical terms. But even so simple an action as voting cannot be understood as merely a physical activity. Imagine how voting might be perceived by an invisible observer from Mars who knows no human language and hasn't the faintest idea what those peculiar earthlings are doing when they enter an enclosed booth and pull a little lever or scratch some black marks on a piece of paper. For all the Martian knows, a person who votes and a person who makes a call from a telephone booth are performing similar acts.

The incompleteness of purely external, physical descriptions of human activity, combined with the difficulty of arriving at an adequate understanding of the subjective features that give human action so much of its meaning, have led some scholars to the pessimistic view that a "scientific" understanding of human action is impossible. Others optimistically view the problems posed as difficult but not insuperable. The pessimistic view suffers from the usual weakness of perfectionism. In this case, the perfectionist appears to be saying that there is nothing worthwhile between utter ignorance, at one extreme, and knowledge of regularities as exhibited in the laws of physics and chemistry, at the other. This is absurd. Some reduction in our uncertainty is better than total uncertainty. No one seriously argues that systematic inquiry can never improve our knowledge, thus reducing our uncertainty.

It is true, however, that uncertainty appears to be a prime characteristic of all political life. Systematic political analysis can reduce some of that uncertainty. Yet even the best political analysis leaves a large element of uncertainty in our understanding of political life. For the foreseeable future, perhaps the only certainty about political life will be its uncertainty. Hence, intelligent political analysis will have to be based on the assumption that political knowledge has distinct limits, even though these are not permanent.

In the following chapters, we shall encounter a number of the factors that create uncertainties in our political knowledge. In Chapter 10, I shall suggest ways of coping with uncertainty in developing policies.

THE PLAN OF THIS BOOK

As I said a moment ago, in the chapters that follow, we begin with some questions that mainly require a clarification of meaning: What is politics? (Chapter 2). What do we mean by political influence and power? (Chapter 3). And what are the main forms of influence? (Chapter 4).

We then proceed to several basic questions that are primarily empirical: In what important ways are all political systems alike? (Chapter 5). In what important ways do they differ? (Chapter 6). What conditions are favorable for the existence of democracy, and conversely, what conditions are unfavorable? (Chapter 7). These three questions require us to analyze large-scale political systems, such as governments of entire countries—what political scientists sometimes call macroanalysis. Our fourth empirical question, however, descends to the level of individuals, or as political scientists say, to microanalysis: How do different people tend to behave in politics? (Chapter 8).

Empirical questions like these may lead one to wonder about the value of different kinds of political arrangements. Most Americans assume that democracy is the best political system and hold, if only vaguely, democratic beliefs. But how can we know what is best in politics? Is believing in democracy merely a matter of taste or prejudice, like preferring vanilla to pistachio ice cream? Or can we choose rationally and wisely among alternative ideologies and political philosophies? How? Normative questions like these are the concern of Chapter 9.

Finally, even assuming that we possess some broad framework of values with which to make judgments, how can we choose wisely among alternative policies, particularly given our uncertain knowledge? This is the subject of Chapter 10.

These questions are endowed with the childlike simplicity found in humanity's persistent questions of life. They are easy to pose, enormously difficult to answer. This book does not furnish the answers. Instead, it provides a few of the analytical tools needed to search for the answers in an intelligent way.

2

WHAT IS POLITICS?

NATURE OF THE POLITICAL ASPECT

What distinguishes the political aspect of human society from other aspects? What are the characteristics of a political system as distinct, say, from an economic system? Although students of politics have never entirely agreed on answers to these questions, they tend to agree on certain key points. Probably no one would quarrel with the notion that a political system is a pattern of political relationships. But what is a political relationship?

On this question, as on many others, an important, though not always entirely clear, place to start is Aristotle's *Politics* (written ca. 335–332 B.C.) In the first book of the *Politics*, Aristotle argues against those who say that all kinds of authority are identical and seeks to distinguish the authority of the political leader in a political association, or polis, from other forms of authority, such as the master over the slave, the husband over the wife, and the parents over the children.

Aristotle takes for granted, however, that at least one aspect of a political association is the existence of *authority* or *rule*. Indeed, Aristotle defines the polis, or political association, as the "most sovereign and inclusive association" and a constitution, or polity, as "the organization of a polis, in respect of its offices generally, but especially in respect of that particular office which is sovereign in all issues."[1] One of Aristotle's criteria for classifying constitutions is the portion of the citizen body in which final *authority* or *rule* is located.

Ever since Aristotle's time, the notion has been widely shared that a political relationship in some way involves authority, ruling, or power. For example, one of the most influential modern social scientists, the German scholar Max Weber (1864–1920), postulated that an association should be called political "if and in so far as the enforcement of its order is carried out continually within a given territorial area by the application and threat of physical force on the part of the administrative staff." Thus, although Weber emphasized the territorial aspect of a political association, like Aristotle he specified that a relationship of authority or rule was one of its essential characteristics.[2]

To take a final example, a leading modern political scientist, Harold Lasswell, defines "political science, as an empirical discipline, [as] the study of the shaping and sharing of power" and "a political act [as] one performed in power perspectives."[3]

The areas of agreement and disagreement in the positions held by Aristotle, Weber, and Lasswell on the nature of politics are illustrated by Figure 2–1. Aristotle, Weber, and Lasswell, and almost all other political scientists, agree that political relationships are to be found somewhere within circle A, the set of relationships involving power, rule, or authority. Lasswell calls everything in A political, by definition. Aristotle and Weber, on the other hand, define the term *political* so as to require one or more additional characteristics, indicated by circles B and C. For example, to Weber the domain of the political would not be everything inside A or everything inside B (territoriality) but everything in the area of overlap, AB, involving both rule *and* territoriality. Although Aristotle is less clear than either Weber or Lasswell on the point, doubtless he would limit the domain of the political even further—to relationships in associations capable of self-sufficiency (C). Hence, to Aristotle, "politics" would be found only in the area ABC.

Clearly, everything that Aristotle and Weber would call political, Lasswell would too. But Lasswell would consider as political some things that Weber and Aristotle might not: A business firm or a trade union, for example, would have "political" aspects. Let us therefore boldly define a political

[1] Ernest Barker, ed., *The Politics of Aristotle* (New York: Oxford University Press, 1962), pp. 1, 110.

[2] Max Weber, *The Theory of Social and Economic Organization*, trans. A. M. Henderson and Talcott Parsons (New York: Oxford University Press, 1947), pp. 145–54.

[3] Harold D. Lasswell and Abraham Kaplan, *Power and Society* (New Haven: Yale University Press, 1950), pp. xiv, 240.

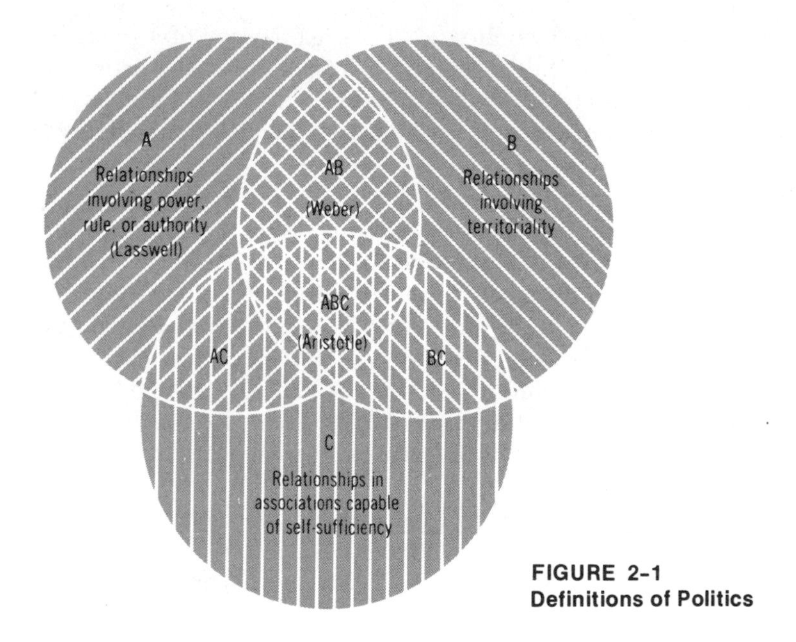

FIGURE 2-1
Definitions of Politics

system as *any persistent pattern of human relationships that involves, to a significant extent, control, influence, power, or authority.*[4]

THE UBIQUITY OF POLITICS

Admittedly, this definition is very broad. Indeed, it means that many associations that most people ordinarily do not regard as "political" possess political systems: private clubs, business firms, labor unions, religious organizations, civic groups, primitive tribes, clans, perhaps even families. Three considerations may help clarify the unfamiliar notion that almost every human association has a political aspect:

(1) In common parlance we speak of the "government" of a club, a firm, and so on. In fact, we may even describe such a government as dictatorial, democratic, representative, or authoritarian; and we often hear about "politics" and "politicking" going on in these associations.

(2) A political system is only *one* aspect of an association. When we say that a person is a doctor, or a teacher, or a farmer, we do not assume that he or she is *only* a doctor, *only* a teacher, *only* a farmer. No human association is exclusively political in all its aspects. People experience many relationships

[4] In Chapter 4, words such as control, power, influence, and authority are called *influence-terms*. The concept of influence is defined in that chapter.

other than power and authority: love, respect, dedication, shared beliefs, and so on.

(3) Our definition says virtually nothing about human *motives.* It definitely does not imply that in every political system people are driven by powerful inner needs to rule others, that leaders passionately want authority, or that politics is inherently a fierce struggle for power. Conceivably, relationships of authority could exist even among people of whom none had a passion for power, or in situations where people who most ardently thirsted for authority had the least chance of acquiring it. Thus the Zuni Indians of the American Southwest are reported to have had a very strong sense that power-seeking was illicit and power-seekers must not be given power.[5] Closer to our own experience is the not uncommon view among members of various American private organizations that those who want most intensely to head the organization are least suited to do so, while the most suitable are among those who least want the job. But whatever the evidence from anthropology or folklore may be, the central point is this: Our highly general definition of a political system makes practically no assumptions as to the nature of human motives. Despite its breadth, the definition helps us make some critical distinctions that are often blurred in ordinary discussions.

(4) Our definition also deliberately ignores a quality that many political philosophers from Aristotle to the present have attributed to politics: that it is in some sense a *public* activity that involves public purposes, or public interests, or a public good, or some other distinctly "public" aspect of human life. If politics were so defined, then we should be obliged to add a fourth circle to Figure 2–1, and the domain of politics would shrink even further. But there are good reasons for not including this notion in our definition, for venerable though it may be among political philosophers, it bristles with difficulties. Some of these can be made clear by considering the orientations mentioned in the first chapter. Is the notion of politics as a public activity intended to be a semantic, an empirical, or a normative interpretation—or some combination? To begin with, this understanding of the meaning of "politics" reflects poorly how the term is used in ordinary language today, where it often refers to the self-seeking and self-promoting activity of ambitious politicians. Likewise, it surely cannot be intended as an empirical account of the *motives* that drive people engaged in politics. For to determine what motivates people requires empirical inquiry and cannot be settled simply by definition. Yet neither common experience nor systematic research seem to give much support to the hypothesis that people who engage in politics are primarily motivated by a concern for the public good. We return to the question of what motivates political man in Chapter 8. If, on the other hand, the notion is not intended to be either a definition or an empirical statement but an assertion of what *ought to be* the end, aim, or result of political

[5] Ruth Benedict, *Patterns of Culture* (Boston: Houghton Mifflin Co., 1934).

life, then it obviously is a normative statement. But as an assertion about ends or values, it requires examination, and cannot reasonably be smuggled in simply as a way of defining politics. In Chapter 9, we return to the problem of political values.

Politics and Economics

Political analysis deals with power, rule or authority. Economics concerns itself with scarce resources or the production and distribution of goods and services. Politics is one aspect of a great variety of human institutions; economics is another aspect. Hence an economist and a political scientist might both study the same concrete institution—the Federal Reserve system, for example, or the budget. But the economist would be concerned primarily with problems involving scarcity and the use of scarce resources, and the political scientist would deal primarily with problems involving relationships of power, rule, or authority. Like most distinctions between subjects of intellectual inquiry, however, that between politics and economics is not perfectly sharp.

Political Systems and Economic Systems

Many people indiscriminately apply terms like *democracy*, *dictatorship*, *capitalism*, and *socialism* to both political and economic systems. This tendency to confuse political with economic systems stems from the lack of a standardized set of definitions, from ignorance of the historical origins of these terms, and in some cases from a desire to exploit a highly favorable or unfavorable political term like "democracy" or "dictatorship" in order to influence attitudes toward economic systems.

It follows, however, that the political aspects of an institution are not the same as its economic aspects. Historically, the terms "democracy" and "dictatorship" usually have referred to political systems, whereas "capitalism" and "socialism" have referred to economic institutions. From the way the terms have been used historically, the following definitions are appropriate:

1. A democracy is a political system in which the opportunity to participate in decisions is widely shared among all adult citizens.
2. A dictatorship is a political system in which the opportunity to participate in decisions is restricted to a few.
3. Capitalism is an economic system in which most major economic activities are performed by privately owned and controlled firms.
4. Socialism is an economic system in which most major activities are performed by agencies owned by the government or society.

Each pair of terms, democracy-dictatorship, capitalism-socialism, implies a dichotomy, and dichotomies are often unsatisfactory. In fact, many political systems are neither wholly democratic nor wholly dictatorial; in many countries private and governmental operations are mixed together in all sorts of complex ways. In the real world, politics and economics are profoundly intermixed. These mixtures not only demonstrate the shortcomings of the dichotomy "capitalism-socialism" but also emphasize the fact that some institutions and processes can be viewed as part of the economic system for certain purposes and as part of the political system for others. The point to remember is that in spite of, or even because of, this intermixing, it has proved to be intellectually fruitful to distinguish some aspects of life as "economic" and other aspects as "political."

Systems and Subsystems

Any collection of elements that interact in some way with one another can be considered a system: a galaxy, a football team, a legislature, a political party.[6] In thinking about political systems, it is helpful to keep in mind four points that apply to any system:

(1) To call something a system is an abstract way of looking at concrete things. One therefore should be careful not to confuse the concrete thing with the abstract "system." A "system" is an aspect of things in some degree abstracted from reality for purposes of analysis; the circulatory system of a mammal or the personality system of a human being are examples.

(2) In order to determine what lies within a particular system and what lies outside it, we need to specify the *boundaries* of that system. Sometimes this task is fairly easy, as in the case of the solar system or the United States Supreme Court, but often it requires an arbitrary decision. For example, what would we consider to be the boundaries of our two major parties? Would we include only party officials? Or would we also include all those who register as Democrats or Republicans? Or those who identify themselves as one or the other, even though they do not register? Or those who vote regularly for the one party or the other? Later on, I shall offer one definition of the boundaries of a political system.

(3) One system can be an element, a subsystem, of another. The earth is a subsystem of our solar system, which is a subsystem of our galaxy, which is a subsystem of the universe. The Foreign Relations Committee is a subsystem of the United States Senate, which is a subsystem of the Congress, and so on.

(4) Something may be a subsystem of two or more different systems that overlap only in part. A college professor might be an active member of the American Association of University Professors, the Democratic party, and the PTA.

[6] The most extensive attempt to apply systems theory to political science is in two works by David Easton: *A Framework for Political Analysis* (Englewood Cliffs, N.J.: Prentice-Hall, Inc. 1965) and *A Systems Analysis of Political Life* (New York: John Wiley & Sons, Inc. 1965).

It is useful to keep these observations in mind in considering the difference between a political system and a social system.

Political Systems and Social Systems

What is a democratic society? a free society? a socialist society? an authoritarian society? an international society? In what way is a social system distinguished from a political system?

Questions like these are particularly difficult to answer because the terms *society* and *social system* are used loosely, even by social scientists. In general, however, the term *social* is intended to be inclusive; economic and political relations are specific kinds of social relations. Although *social system* is sometimes given a more specific meaning, it too is a broad concept. Thus, Talcott Parsons, a leading American sociologist, defined a social system by three characteristics: (1) two or more persons interact; (2) in their actions they take account of how the others are likely to act; and (3) sometimes they act together in pursuit of common goals.[7] A social system, then, is a very inclusive kind of order.

According to Parsons's usage, a political system or an economic system would be parts, aspects, or subsystems of a social system. This way of looking at the matter is illustrated in Figure 2–2, where AC represents the set of all

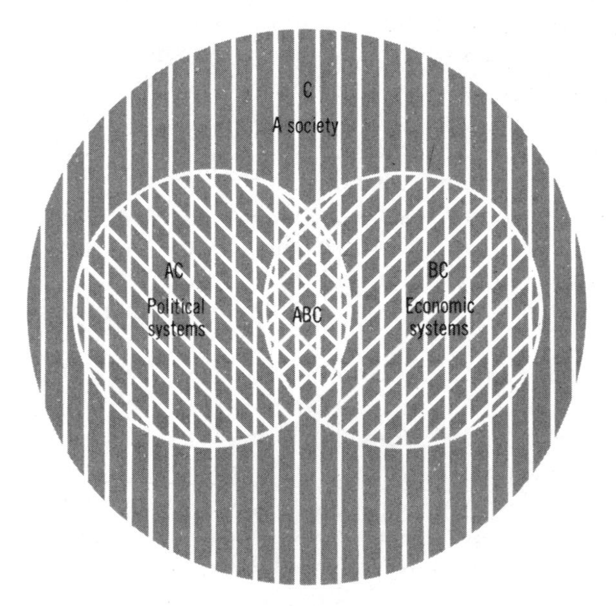

FIGURE 2-2
Society, Political Systems, Economic Systems

[7] Talcott Parsons and Edward A. Shils, eds., *Toward a General Theory of Action* (Cambridge, Mass.: Harvard University Press, 1951), p. 55. For a discussion of the meaning and history of the concept "society," see *International Encyclopedia of the Social Sciences*, s.v. "society."

political subsystems and ABC represents subsystems that can be considered as either political or economic, depending on which aspect we are concerned with. Examples of ABC would be General Motors, the Budget Committee of the United States Senate, or the Board of Governors of the Federal Reserve System.

Thus, a democratic *society* could be defined as a social system that has not only democratic political (sub)systems but also a number of other subsystems that operate to contribute directly or indirectly to the strength of the democratic political processes. Conversely, by definition, an authoritarian society would contain many important subsystems, such as the family, the churches, and the schools, all acting to strengthen authoritarian political processes. Let us consider two examples.

In his famous *Democracy in America* (1835–1840) the illustrious French writer Alexis de Tocqueville listed a number of "principal causes which tend to maintain the democratic republic in the United States." His list included not only the constitutional structure but also the absence of a large military establishment, equality in social and economic conditions, a prosperous agricultural economy, and the mores, customs, and religious beliefs of Americans.[8] In Tocqueville's view the prospects for a healthy democratic *political* system in the United States were strengthened enormously by the fact that a highly democratic Constitution was reinforced by many other aspects of the *society*. Hence American society could be called a democratic society.

By contrast, many observers were pessimistic about the prospects of democracy in Germany after World War II because they believed that many aspects of German society were highly authoritarian and tended to undermine democratic political relations. They were mainly concerned with the wide tendency for social institutions of all kinds to take on a strong pattern of dominance and submission—the family, schools, churches, business, and all relations between government officials, whether police or civil servants, and ordinary citizens. The fact that political democracy had to be instituted in a predominantly authoritarian social environment was not particularly auspicious for the future of democracy in Germany. A number of recent observers, on the other hand, feel optimistic about the future of political democracy in Germany now precisely because they see evidence that the authoritarian character of other social institutions has greatly declined.

Government and State

In every society, people tend to develop more or less standard expectations about social behavior in various situations. One learns how to behave as a host or a guest, a parent or grandparent, a "good loser," a soldier, a bank

[8] Alexis de Tocqueville, *Democracy in America*, vol. 1 (New York: Vintage Books, 1955), pp. 298–342.

clerk, a prosecutor, a judge, and so on. Patterns like these, in which a number of people share roughly similar expectations about behavior in particular situations, are called *roles*. We all play various roles and frequently shift from one role to another rapidly.

Whenever a political system is complex and stable, political roles develop. Perhaps the most obvious political roles are played by persons who create, interpret, and enforce rules that are binding on members of the political system. These roles are *offices*, and the collection of offices in a political system constitutes the government of that system. At any given moment, of course, these offices, or roles, are (aside from vacancies) filled by particular individuals, concrete persons—Senator Foghorn, Judge Cranky, Mayor Twimbly. But in many systems the roles remain much the same even when they are played by a succession of individuals. To be sure, different actors may—and usually do—interpret the role of Hamlet or Othello in different ways, sometimes in radically different ways. So, too, with political roles. Jefferson, Jackson, Lincoln, Theodore Roosevelt, Wilson, and Franklin Roosevelt, for example, each enlarged the role of President beyond what he had inherited from his predecessors by building new expectations in people's minds about what a President should or legitimately could do in office. "There are as many different ways of being President," Nelson Polsby asserts, "as there are men willing to fill the office."[9] Yet expectations as to the proper role of the President also limit the extent to which they can make it what they wish—a fact dramatized by President Johnson's decision in 1968 not to seek reelection because, in effect, he could no longer play the presidential role in the way that he believed the office required.

But—a reader might ask—in defining *government* as we have just done, don't we create a new problem for ourselves? If there is a great variety of political systems—from trade unions and universities to countries and international organizations—what about *the* Government? After all, the United States, as in most other countries, when you speak of *the* Government everyone seems to know what you mean. Of all the governments in the various associations of a particular territory, generally one is in some way recognized as *the* Government. How does *the* Government differ from other governments? Consider three possible answers:

(1) *The* Government pursues "higher" and "nobler" purposes than other governments. There are at least three difficulties with this proposal. First, because people disagree about what the "higher" or "nobler" purposes are, and even whether a given purpose is or is not being pursued at any given moment, this criterion might not be very helpful in trying to decide whether

[9] See N. Polsby's *Congress and the Presidency* 3rd. ed. (Englewood Cliffs, N.J.: Prentice-Hall, Inc., 1976). Polsby compares the presidents from Franklin Roosevelt to Gerald Ford. See also James David Barber, *The Presidential Character: Predicting Performance in the White House* (Englewood Cliffs, N.J.: Prentice-Hall, Inc., 1972).

this or that government is *the* Government. Second, despite the fact that people often disagree over how to rank purposes or values and may even hold that *the* Government is pursuing evil ends, they still agree on what is and what is not *the* Government. An anarchist does not doubt that he is being oppressed by *the* Government. Third, what about bad Governments? For example, do democratic and totalitarian governments *both* pursue noble purposes? That point seems logically absurd.

Our first proposed answer, then, confuses the problem of defining Government with the more difficult and more important task of deciding on the criteria for a "good" or "just" Government. Before we can decide what the *best* Government is, we must know first what *the* Government is.

(2) Aristotle suggested another possibility: *The* Government is distinguished by the character of the association to which it pertains—namely, a political association that is self-sufficient, in the sense that it possesses all the qualities and resources necessary for a good life. This definition suffers from some of the same difficulties as the first. Moreover, if it were strictly applied, we should have to conclude that no Governments exist! Aristotle's idealized interpretation of the city-state was very far from reality even in his day. Athens was not self-sufficient culturally, economically, or militarily. In fact, it was quite unable to guarantee its own peace or independence; without allies, it could not even maintain the freedom of its own citizens. What was true of the Greek city-states is of course equally true today.

(3) *The* Government is any government that successfully upholds a claim to the exclusive regulation of the legitimate use of physical force in enforcing its rules within a given territorial area.[10] The political system made up of the residents of that territorial area and the Government of the area is a *State*.[11]

This definition immediately suggests three questions:

(1) Can't individuals who aren't Government officials ever legitimately use force? What about parents who spank their children? The answer is, of course, that the Government of a State does not necessarily *monopolize* the use of force, but it has the exclusive authority to set the limits within which force may legitimately be used. The Governments of most States permit private individuals to use force in some circumstances. For example, although many Governments forbid cruel or excessive punishment of children, most permit parents to spank their own offspring. Boxing is permitted in many countries.

(2) What about criminals who go uncaught? After all, no country is free

[10] Adapted from Weber, *Theory of Social and Economic Organization*, p. 154, by substituting "exclusive regulation" for "monopoly" and "rules" for "its order."

[11] Capitalized here to avoid confusion with constituent states in federal systems.

of assault, murder, rape, and other forms of violence and criminals sometimes escape the law. The point is, however, that the claim of the Government of the State to regulate violence and force is successfully upheld, in the sense that few people would seriously contest the exclusive right of the State to punish criminals. Although criminal violence exists, it is not legitimate.

(3) What about circumstances of truly widespread violence and force, such as civil war or revolution? In this case no single answer will suffice. For brief periods, no State may exist at all, since no government is capable of upholding its claim to the exclusive regulation of the legitimate use of physical force. Several governments may contest for the privilege over the same territory. Or what was formerly a territory ruled by the Government of one State may now be divided and ruled by the Governments of two or more States, with gray stateless areas where they meet.

We can be reasonably sure of one thing: When large numbers of people in a particular territory begin to doubt or deny the claim of the Government to regulate force, then the existing State is in peril of dissolution.

3
POLITICAL INFLUENCE

Few matters can be more complex than power, and few are more often so grossly oversimplified. The tendency to drastic oversimplification is probably fueled by a desire to make at least some sense out of the enormous complexity of power and influence.

Let me offer an example. Many people have definite and simple ideas about the influence of business on government. However, a Dutch scholar who investigated the influence of business firms on the Dutch government produced a book of 211 pages of text and appendices—and focused on only a small sub-set of Dutch firms! While you might attribute such detail to academic fussiness and verbosity, the book is actually quite closely reasoned and the evidence is parsimoniously laid out. Even so, one could reasonably object that he has considerably oversimplified the relations between business and government in the Netherlands.[1]

How can the analysis of power and influence be so complex? Can we

[1] Geert P. A. Braam, *Influence of Business Firms on the Government, An Investigation of the Distribution of Influence in Society* (The Hague: Mouton, 1981). Among his principal findings are: 1. Government decision-making does not favor large firms over small firms. 2. However, small firms saw themselves as having fewer problems than larger firms. 3. Organizations and associations of firms are effective in promoting the interests of their members in relation to the government, but they are also very likely a cause of new social inequalities because of differences in the involvement of members in the organizations.

avoid excessive oversimplification and still make some sense out of the confusion and complexity of power?

THE ABSENCE OF STANDARD TERMINOLOGY

"Control," "power," "influence," and "authority" are words not exclusive to political practitioners and political theorists. One hears of the power to govern, the power of the purse, spiritual power, economic power, national power, presidential power, and Black Power.

Thus we all speak of power and assume that others know what we mean. The concept of power, as we saw in the last chapter, is central to political analysis; the notion of politics and a political system presupposes that words like control, power, authority, and influence have a definite meaning. The fact is, however, that these words are ambiguous; their meaning is elusive and complex.

With words like power and influence, neither in ordinary language nor in political science is there agreement on terms and definitions. Like others, political scientists use a variety of terms: power, influence, authority, control, persuasion, might, force, coercion. Let us, for convenience, simply call these "influence-terms." Like others, political scientists frequently do not define these terms; and when they do, they do not agree with each other. Although influence-terms have been central to political analysis throughout history, most theorists seem to have assumed, as did Aristotle, that they needed no great elaboration, presumably because their meaning would be understood by people of common sense.[2] Even Machiavelli, who was fascinated by the play of power, used a variety of undefined terms to describe and explain political life. In fact, the last several decades probably have witnessed more systematic efforts to tie down these concepts than have the previous millennia of political thought.[3] As a result, there has been a vast improvement in the clarity of the concepts. Yet it is still true that writers do not use influence-terms in the same way: one writer's "influence" is another's "power." For the time being, I shall use these terms as if they were interchangeable.

THREE FALLACIES IN THE ANALYSIS OF POWER

The Lump-of-Power Fallacy. Power is thought of often as if it were a single, solid, unbreakable lump. The lump can be passed from one actor to

[2] An interesting attempt to clarify the meaning of various influence-terms by analyzing their usage in "ordinary" language (actually the language of highly educated writers) will be found in Hanna Pitkin, *Wittgenstein and Justice* (Berkley: University of California, 1972), pp. 276 ff.

[3] References will be found on pp. 146–147.

another, but cannot be shared. Either one has *the* power or one has *no* power. Presumably this is the notion that many people, in particular journalists, hold when they ask, "Who has the power around here?"

In contrast to wealth, income, social status, and other matters of value, many people do not conceive of power as a variable with a number of possible values. To them it has only two values: 0 or 1. Because wealth or income can take on many values—10 cents, $5.00, $35,000, $3 million, and so on—one can imagine different ways in which it might be distributed among the members of a group. When power is thought of as a lump, however, it can be distributed in only one way: Some have all the power, and the rest have none.[4]

But in society and politics things rarely fall neatly into two and only two piles, and two-fold, mutually exclusive classification schemes—dichotomies—are often misleading. An effort to treat wealth, income, or status in a dichotomous manner would impose an absurd and unnecessary handicap on our capacity to describe the way in which these are distributed, say, in the United States. Although the difficulties of measuring power are great, there is no reason why power, authority, control, or influence need to be conceived of in this fashion.

Confounding Power with Resources. Compare these two statements:

> Money is influence.
>
> In deciding to increase milk subsidies, the President was influenced by the milk producers, because they had contributed heavily to his campaign.

In the first statement, money and influence appear to be equivalent. Or perhaps money is conceived of as one kind of influence. Is the intention, then, to define influence? If so, wherever the term influence occurs, we could simply substitute the word money. Should we try to do so, however, we would quickly see that the substitution leads to confusion and even absurdity.

[4] The lump-of-power fallacy occurs even in important works in social theory. A leading example is Ralf Dahrendorf's influential book *Class and Class Conflict in Industrial Society* (Stanford, Calif.: Stanford University Press, 1956), pp. 166–67, 171–73. See also the definitions 2.1, 2.1.1, and 2.1.2 on p. 237. Dahrendorf adds the following highly important qualification at p. 173, which, however, entirely drops out of his account: "This is not to say, of course, that there is no difference between those who have a great deal and those who have merely a little authority. Among the positions of domination there may be, and often is, considerable differentiation. But such differentiation, *while important for empirical analysis*, leaves unaffected the existence of a border line somewhere between those who have whatever little authority and the 'outs.' Strictly speaking, an analytical statement which states that there is a dichotomy of authority positions is tautological; but as this example shows, there are tautologies which are worth stating." [Emphasis added] One might add: tautologies may be worth stating, but they are hardly worth presenting as the crucial assumption of an empirical theory. For another example, in which the author explicitly follows Dahrendorf's lead, see I. Balbus, "The Concept of Interest in Pluralist and Marxist Analysis," *Politics and Society* 1 (February 1971):151–77.

Additionally, it would fail to catch the full meaning of what we wanted to say. Consider, for example,

> The President has a great deal of influence over Congress when it makes decisions as to the level of military spending.

Suppose we try to substitute "money" for "influence":

> The President has a great deal of money . . . over Congress? . . . in dealing with Congress? . . . for influencing Congress? . . .

Something has gone wrong. We don't quite know how to complete the sentence without either changing the meaning of "influence" or destroying the supposed equivalence of "money" and "influence."

When we simply define influence or power as equivalent to resources, we not only lose specificity as to subject matter but also we ignore an important empirical problem—whether and how the relation of influence is to be explained by the way in which one of the actors in the relationship uses resources. We simply deal with the problem of explanation by fiat: We assert a relationship, but we do not investigate it, let alone try to demonstrate it.

Confounding Power With Rewards and Deprivations. Consider the following:

[a] Because they had contributed heavily to his campaign,
[b] the President was influenced by the milk producers,
[c] in deciding to increase milk subsidies. As a result,
[d] the incomes of the milk producers were increased.

Notice that [d] is a *consequence* of [c], the President's decision (and therefore indirectly a consequence of [a] and [b]). The President's decision helps to explain the increase in the incomes of the milk producers, just as [a] helps to explain [b] and [c]. These relationships are shown in Figure 3–1.

If we were to define influence or power as exactly equivalent to its consequences for the allocation of rewards and deprivations, we once again would deal with empirical questions by fiat. We would not demonstrate a relationship, we would proclaim it. It might be supposed that the existence of a difference between an influence-relationship [b] with respect to certain kinds of decisions or outcomes [c], and the consequences of that relationship for rewards and deprivations [d] is so obvious that no one would confound the two. Unfortunately that is not so. Important works in social theory do sometimes confound the two.[5]

[5] For example, see Frank Parkin, *Class Inequality and Political Order* (New York: Holt, Rinehart & Winston, 1971), p. 46. Earlier, Parkin seems to commit the lump-of-power fallacy (p. 26).

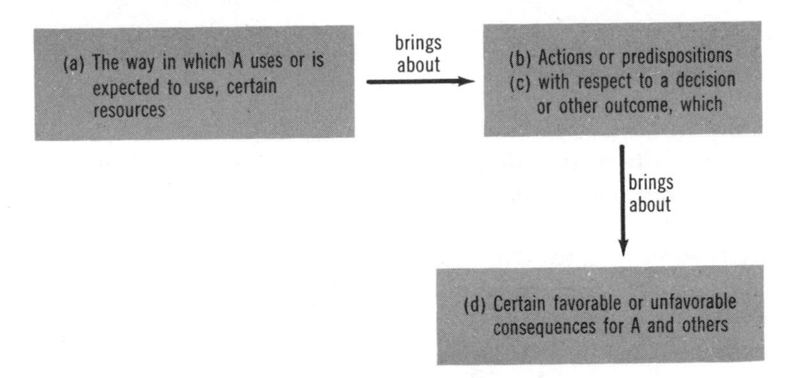

FIGURE 3-1 Distinguishing Power from its Consequences

WHAT WE MEAN BY INFLUENCE

There is general agreement that influence-terms refer to relationships among human beings. I may speak of human power over nature or my power over my dog; a theologian may speak of God's power, or divine influence on events. But in political analysis, influence terms are usually restricted to relationships among human actors.

For the moment, we can capture the meaning of one general type of human relationship that might be called *manifest* or *explicit* influence. Suppose you were to stand on a street corner and say to yourself, "I command all automobile drivers on this street to drive on the right-hand side of the road"; suppose also that all the drivers actually did as you "commanded" them to do. Most people would regard you as mentally ill if you were to insist that you had just shown enough influence over automobile drivers to compel them to use the right-hand side of the road. On the other hand, suppose a police officer stands in the middle of an intersection at which most traffic ordinarily moves ahead and orders all traffic to turn right or left. The traffic moves right or left as ordered. Then common sense suggests that the officer acting in this particular role influences automobile drivers to turn right or left rather than go ahead.

Our common sense notion, then, goes something like this: Suppose there are only two people in a system, A and B. A influences B to the extent that he or she changes B's actions or predispositions in some way.

Power as Cause

To clarify the notion of influence by appealing to common sense understandings, I have used terms like "induce," "cause," and "bring about." Consequently, a number of writers have suggested that influence be defined as a special kind of causal relation: Thus the expression "A influences B to do x" could be recast as "A causes B to do x."[6]

Yet suppose that Albert and Betty are walking along the sidewalk, Albert accidentally bumps Betty, and Betty drops her packages. It is certainly correct to say that Albert (unintentionally) *caused* Betty to drop her packages, but we would not ordinarily say that Albert *influenced* Betty to drop her packages. If Albert really wanted Betty to drop her packages, perhaps to embarrass her, or to steal her packages, or to play a joke, or to introduce himself—in any of these cases we should be inclined to say that Albert influenced Betty to drop her packages.

It appears, then, that when we single out influence from all the other aspects of a human interaction in order to give it special attention, what interests us and what we focus attention on is that one or more of the persons in this interaction get what they want, or at least get closer to what they want, by causing other people to act in some particular way. We want to call attention to a *causal relationship* between what A wants and what B does. Recently, Nagel has proposed a formulation that specifically emphasizes these features, which, paraphrased, states:

> Influence is a relation among actors such that the wants, desires, preferences, or intentions of one or more actors affect the actions, or predispositions to act, of one or more other actors.[7]

Manifest and Implicit Influence

Nagel has shown that a definition of influence along these lines enables one to deal with a long-standing difficulty more successfully than definitions that

[6] Because Bertrand Russell and several other philosophers attempted several generations ago to dismiss causal explanation as unnecessary in science, some analysts have been timid about treating causation as civilly as I do here. However, Russell's attempt to banish causation from the vocabulary of science was unsuccessful. Whatever may be the case with the formal vocabulary of physics, the physicist cannot carry on experiments and the rest of us cannot act upon the world without some concept of causation. For a philosophical treatment of cause germane to human action, see Georg Henrik von Wright. *Explanation and Understanding* (Ithaca, N.Y.: Cornell University Press, 1971).

[7] Nagel's definition of power is: "A power relation, actual or potential, is an actual or potential causal relation between the preferences of an actor regarding an outcome and the outcome itself." Jack H. Nagel, *The Descriptive Analysis of Power* (New Haven: Yale University Press, 1975), p. 29. Nagel himself sees "no reason not to apply the definition . . . to power of human actors over nonsocial outcomes (e.g., the weather)" (fn. 16, p. 29). I believe, however, that in political analysis the definition will be more useful if it is restricted to "social outcomes," that is, to relationships involving human actors. In any case, that is how it is used in this book. Nagel's emphasis on the causal aspects of influence is not original, nor does he claim so. In 1953, Herbert A. Simon advanced this idea in his influential "Notes on the Observation and Measurement of Political Power," *Journal of Politics* 15 (1953):500–516. In the same year C. E. Lindblom and I, using the term *control* where Simon used *power*, wrote: "In loose language, A controls the responses of B if A's acts cause B to respond in a definite way." *Politics, Economics, and Welfare* (New York: Harper & Brothers, 1953), p. 94. However, believing that the concept of causation was itself unclear, I usually preferred other language. Nagel's contribution is to show more fully and rigorously than previous writers the implications and uses of a causal conception of influence.

had been proposed previously: the problem of A's implicit influence over B arising from *anticipations* by B as to what A wants. The nature of implicit influence can be made clearer if we first distinguish it from manifest influence:

> If A wants outcome x; if A acts with the intention of causing B to bring about x; and if as a result of A's actions, B attempts to bring about x, then A exercises *manifest* influence over B.

Manifest influence is easier to detect than implicit influence arising from anticipations. The "rule of anticipated reactions" was introduced by Friedrich in 1937[8] to refer to a situation in which "one actor, B, shapes his behavior to conform to what he believes are the desires of another actor, A, without having received explicit messages about A's wants or intentions from A or A's agents."[9]

Friedrich offered examples to show that if one were to concentrate attention exclusively on manifest influence, one would often underestimate or entirely miss the influence of an important actor, such as the influence of the British Parliament on the conduct of foreign affairs by the foreign Office.[10] Without taking anticipations into account, one would find it difficult to explain the full effects of elections on elected officials or of business on government.[11] To the extent that elected officials are guided by the outcome of the preceding election, they are manifestly influenced by voters; to the extent that they are guided by a desire to be reelected and by expectations of future reactions of voters or campaign contributors to their present conduct, then they are subject to the implicit influence of voters and campaign contributors. Earlier definitions made it difficult to deal with instances like these, in which influence is mediated by anticipated reactions. Now, however, we can define implicit influence in a fashion consistent with the general definition of influence given before:

> If A wants outcome x, then although A does not act with the intention of causing B to bring about x, if A's desire for x causes B to attempt to bring about x, then A exercises implicit influence over B.

Although formally it will do the job, the language of this definition is formidable. Another example may help. Until Wilbur Mills resigned his

[8] Carl J. Friedrich, *Constitutional Government and Democracy* (New York: Harper & Brothers, 1937), pp. 16–18.

[9] Nagel, *Analysis of Power*, p. 16

[10] Carl J. Friedrich, *Man and His Government* (New York: McGraw-Hill Book Co., 1963), pp. 201–2.

[11] Charles E. Lindblom contends that in countries with privately owned, market-oriented economic systems, business people enjoy a "privileged" position because in order to ensure their performance at satisfactory levels, governments must provide them with inducements in the form of a great variety of rewards. Cf *Politics and Markets* (New York: Basic Books, Inc., Publishers, 1977), pp. 170–200.

chairmanship shortly after his reelection in 1974 in the wake of a personal scandal, he was widely acknowledged to be one of the most influential members of the Congress because of his key role as Chairman of the House Committee on Ways and Means, which has jurisdiction over all tax legislation. That Mills was highly influential within his committee is hardly open to doubt. Nor can it be questioned that the decisions of the committee, in turn, had enormous influence on the prospects in the Congress for action on tax matters.[12] Yet it appears that the committee and the House also had considerable influence over Mills.

As to the House, after one of the first major bills Mills took to the floor was voted down, he was always exceedingly cautious to avoid bringing out a bill that might be defeated. Because of his effort to anticipate the reactions of the House, the members of that body exercised implicit influence over Mills. Moreover, within his committee he was a persistent and industrious seeker after consensus. The author of a study of the committee remarks: "The essence of a consensus-seeking form of leadership, the kind practiced by Mills, is mutual dependence, a relationship between Mills and the committee that involves the flow of influence from the committee to Mills just as much as the flow from Mills to the committee."[13] Thus, the committee's influence on Mills was a mixture of both manifest and implicit influence.

WHAT WE MEAN BY MORE INFLUENCE

Now that we have seen why a causal definition along the lines just set out seems best suited to our purpose, we must confront a major problem: how to describe the relative influence of different actors in a political system, or of the same actor in different times or circumstances.

An analogy may help. Economists, census-takers, and policy-makers often want to know how income and wealth are distributed in a country. How great is income inequality in the United States? How much, if at all, do taxes change the distribution of income? Is the gap in incomes between white and blacks decreasing? Between men and women in the labor force?

In measuring income, one great advantage economists have is the existence of money as a medium of exchange. Although money provides a convenient unit for measuring income, it is not a perfect measure of everything that might constitute income. Nevertheless, for many purposes what we really want to know about is income received in the form of money:

[12] The Committee is widely thought (and expected) to be the master of its esoteric subject matter, and in exchange for this expertise the House voluntarily gives up its right to amend Ways and Means bills . . ." John F. Manley, *The Politics of Finance: The House Committee on Ways and Means* (Boston: Little, Brown & Co., 1970), p. 72.

[13] *Ibid.*, p. 122. See also pp. 105–6, 108.

money income. But how would one go about measuring the relative amount of power or influence of different actors in a system? A satisfactory measure would enable us to determine different amounts of influence in somewhat the same way that test scores are used to determine IQ, degrees to determine temperature, or money to determine income. At a minimum, we could then decide whether Addy's influence was more than Bret's, Bret's more than Calvin's (and thus Addy's more than Calvin's), and so on. Unfortunately, however, no one has yet been able to show how we might meaningfully describe the distribution of influence in the same way that we can describe the distribution of IQ test scores among school children, or yesterday's noon temperature in various cities of the world, or the incomes of American families.[14]

Scope and Domain

The *domain* of an actor's influence consists of the other actors influenced by him or her. The *scope* of an actor's influence refers to the matters on which he or she can influence them. In exercising influence, then, an actor influences a domain of other actors with respect to a certain scope of their actions or predispositions.

We can add up a family's income from different sources—salary, rents, interest, dividends, and so on—to arrive at its total income. We can then add up the total incomes of some category of families—the poorest 25 percent, blacks, the elderly, wage earners—and arrive at an aggregate figure for that category. In the case of influence, however, it is difficult enough to estimate relative influence within a particular scope and domain; it is by no means clear how we can "add up" influence over many different scopes and domains in order to arrive at total, or aggregate, influence.

Any statement about influence that does not clearly indicate the domain and scope it refers to verges on being meaningless. When one hears that A is highly influential, the proper question is: Influential over what actors with respect to what matters? The failure to insist on this simple question often leads political observers astray. For example, several pioneering efforts that helped to trigger off a large number of studies of community power paid scant attention to the possibility that people who are regarded as leaders in a com-

[14] In the technical language of measurement theory, IQ scores provide an *ordinal* scale that allows us only to rank different persons according to their test scores. Degrees of temperature provide an *interval* scale as well, because the intervals between units are assumed to be equal. Therefore, not only can we rank the different cities from cooler to warmer, according to their noon temperatures, but we can also say that the difference between Portland, Maine, (70°) and Portland, Oregon, (60°) was the same as between Chicago (90°) and Washington (100°). Money provides a *ratio* scale because we can not only rank and compare differences but we can also compare ratios, e.g., Amy's annual income of $40,000 is twice as great as Bret's income of $20,000. Although a valid and reliable ordinal scale for comparing influence within a particular scope and domain seems to me the most we can hope for, discussions about power and influence often imply the existence of a higher level of measurement for total influence.

munity might be influential on some matters but not others. As investigators became more concerned with differences in "scopes" of influence, they began to discover that a community leader's influence is often highly specialized: A person influences decisions about schools, let us say, but not about zoning; or a person is influential on urban redevelopment but not on political nominations or elections.[15]

Amount: Within a Given Scope and Domain

The problem of how to "add up" an actor's influence with respect to different scopes, let alone "add up" influence with respect to different scopes over different domains of persons, has proved intractable. If influence is a form of causation, then the amount of A's influence over an outcome should be equivalent to the amount of the outcome (B's actions) or predispositions caused by A's desires. As direct as this approach is, theorists have shied away from it because there are difficulties in measuring the amount of an effect attributable to a supposed cause. A definition along these lines, it appeared, would translate one definition into another, but it would still not offer a way of measuring influence.

Nagel argues, however, that the amount of power, so defined, can be measured by means of sophisticated statistical methods.[16] Unfortunately, however, these methods would require a level of precise measurement that is usually impossible to attain in observing the exercise of influence.[17]

Despite these acute disadvantages, Nagel's proposal for measuring the relative amount of power of different actors has significant value for illuminating and guiding thought and research involving the concept of

[15] Thus a political scientist who studied "The Elites of Atlanta" discovered that a group of fifty-seven persons who were reported by well-informed observers of the Atlanta scene to be influential in making important community decisions were rarely key actors on more than one of three key issues studied. The three issues were a bond program, a mayoralty election, and urban renewal. Of the fifty-seven with a reputation for influence, only twelve were key actors on two issues, and only four were key actors on all three issues. M. Kent Jennings, *Community Influentials: The Elites of Atlanta* (New York: The Free Press, 1964), p. 160, Table 21. I have calculated the figures from percentages in the table.

[16] Nagel, *Analysis of Power*, pp. 55 ff. For a brief discussion of other measures see *ibid.*, Chap. Six, "Measures of Power," pp. 83–99. Nagel shows that a measure I proposed some years ago is a special case of his. See my article "The Concept of Power," *Behavioral Science* 2 (July 1957): 201–15. This has been reprinted together with many other articles on the subject in Roderick Bell, David V. Edwards, and R. Harrison Wagner, eds., *Political Power, a Reader in Theory and Research* (New York: The Free Press, 1969).

[17] Nagel's method requires a statistical technique known as path analysis, which in turn assumes that the variables are measured on interval scales. (Cf. fn. 14, *supra*, p. 27.) As Nagel points out "The appropriateness of path analysis for ordinal data remains a major unsettled issue. . . . The controversy is not one I can resolve, though the use of path analysis with ordinal data is obviously an appealing possibility. An answer is not crucial for the primarily heuristic applications of path analysis in this book. . . . Those who would apply path analysis in empirical power research, however, must take the level of measurement problem into account." *Ibid.*, p. 73.

influence. It boils down to the essential question: How much do the wants or desires of some actors effect the actions or predispositions of others? No matter what techniques one may use to arrive at an answer, if power is conceived of as a kind of causation, then surely this is the right question to ask.

Total Amount of Influence

If one were to use this measure to estimate an actor's influence within a given scope and domain, one still would face the problem of adding an actor's influence in various scopes and domains to arrive at an aggregate. How could we determine, for example, whether the President is, in the aggregate, more powerful than the Congress?

The difficulty is this: There does not appear to be a satisfactory objective method for weighing scopes—for example, foreign policy, taxation, appropriations, public opinion, elections, and so on. Evaluating the relative importance of influence over these areas tends to be arbitrary or subjective. An analogous problem arises when we try to compare two athletes who compete in different sports. Was Babe Ruth a better athlete than Jack Dempsey? The question seems unanswerable. We might measure Babe Ruth against other hitters by using the number of home runs as a measure, and we might measure Dempsey against other fighters by using the number of knockouts, but how do we compare home runs with knockouts? If two athletes were to compete in the same sports, perhaps we could determine that one was a better athlete by comparison. For example, if A were as good a hitter as B in baseball, an equally good boxer, but better in tennis, we might then say that A was a better athlete than B.

In exactly the same way it seems reasonable to say that one actor has more aggregate influence only if A's influence is not less than B's in any issue area and greater in at least one issue area. If Green and Thompson are both highly influential on public school issues and urban redevelopment, but Green is more influential than Thompson on political nominations, then Green is more influential than Thompson in the aggregate.

Real life, however, does not always produce such neatly tailored situations. Green may be more influential than Thompson on school questions, while Thompson may be more influential than Green on political nominations. What do we say in this case? We might try to assign weights to different issue areas, but weights are bound to be arbitrary. If schools are given a weight of 1, what weight should be given to political nominations—2, 5, ½? How can we justify the weights we assign?

It might be thought that the total size of an actor's domain could provide a measure of total power. But we can see that this would lead to absurdities in comparing the total power of different actors, because it would ignore both the amount of power within a given scope and the incomparability of influence within different scopes. Thus, if Green can mobilize 5,000 votes for any candidate she supports and Thompson 10,000, it seems reasonable to say that Thompson's influence on elections is greater than Green's. But suppose that Green can always mobilize 6 votes on the eleven-person city council, while Thompson can mobilize none. It would then be silly to insist that because Thompson's 10,000 votes outnumber Green's 5,000 votes, therefore Thompson's total power is greater than Green's.

There is at present no single best way of solving the problem of comparability when actors have different amounts of influence with respect to different matters. Perhaps the most important lesson the student of politics can gain from this is the need for caution and clarity in making comparisons of influence. As in many other cases, it is wise in political analysis to specify whether we are adding oranges, or apples, or oranges *and* apples.

OBSERVING INFLUENCE

At this point the impatient reader might ask: If these measures are so difficult to apply in practice, how an I ever going to learn anything by trying to observe influence in the real world—in Congress, for example? The answer is that the formal notions of influence and ways of measuring relative influence serve as guides to observation and analysis. They constitute criteria that can rarely be met perfectly and often only crudely.

The best political observers ask essentially those questions suggested by our semantic analysis so far. For example, they may ask: What persons or groups have the greatest effect on congressional legislation of taxes? Who tends to initiate proposals, to win others over to them, to carry them through over opposition, to veto or sidetrack the proposals of others? Why do some questions never become public issues? Although descriptions of patterns of influence were once primarily the province of journalists and historians, the last several decades have seen a flourishing of scholarly efforts by social scientists to study concrete, contemporary systems of influence.

Although most studies have focused more on manifest than on implicit influence, some investigations have observed the importance of anticipated reactions in the electoral process and hence on the influence exercised by voters and campaign contributors over elected officials. Thus Mayhew has shown recently that a substantial amount of the behavior, processes, and policies of members of the United States Congress can be explained adequately by the Representative's or Senator's desire for reelection.[18] Tufte has shown that federal expenditures usually increase during election years and increase more during presidential election years than during the mid-term congressional election years. These election-year increases are not accidental;

[18] David R. Mayhew, *Congress: The Electoral Connection* (New Haven: Yale University Press, 1974).

they result from pressures exerted by the President and his party associates in the Executive Branch and the Congress in order to create a favorable partisan climate for the coming election.[19]

EXPLAINING DIFFERENCES IN INFLUENCE

However crude or imperfect our observations may be, one of the most commonly reported characteristics of all political systems is that political influence is unequally distributed. Why is this so? Assuming that we have observed and described the way influence is distributed among the members of some political system, how could we explain what we had found? In general, differences in the amount of influence that persons exercise can be attributed directly to three fundamental explanatory factors:

1. Differences in the distribution of political resources. A political resource is a means by which one person can influence the behavior of other persons. Political resources therefore include money, information, food, the threat of force, jobs, friendship, social standing, the right to make laws, votes, and a great variety of other things.
2. Variations in the skill or efficiency with which individuals use their political resources. Differences in political skill stem in turn from differences in endowments, opportunities, and incentives to learn and practice political skills.
3. Variations in the extent to which individuals use their resources for political purposes. Of two equally wealthy people, for example, one may use her wealth to gain influence while another may use his to achieve success in business. These variations are themselves traceable to differences in motivation that arise out of variations in endowments and experiences.

The Network of Causes

Thus some key links in the causal network might be illustrated by Figure 3–2. These links are only a part of the network of causation. Other links radiate indefinitely beyond this immediate focus. The analysis of influence is similar to other causal analysis. How do we explain a particular forest fire? If we conclude that it was caused by campers, why did the campers cause the fire? Did they deliberately set it? If so, why did they wish to set fire to the forest? If their action was not deliberate, how do we explain their carelessness? What about other causes? Were the woods unusually dry? If so, why? Shall we also try to explain the peculiar weather? Is this likely to be a long-run cycle? Why didn't the Park Service prevent camping during the dry period?

The links on which we focus attention in a causal explanation depend on

[19] Edward R. Tufte, *Political Control of the Economy* (New Haven: Yale University Press, 1978).

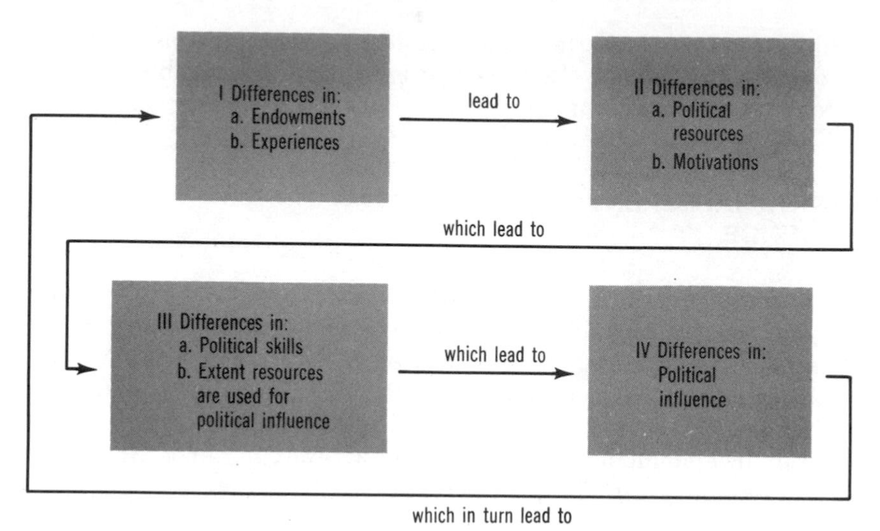

FIGURE 3-2 Some Factors Accounting for Differences in Political Influence

our purposes and interests. Perhaps we want to understand why campers are careless with fires in the hopes that a program of public information or regulation might help. Or we may want to determine how the Park Service can prevent fire. We may also want to consider changing the weather by cloud-seeding during dry periods. If complete analysis required us to trace every cause back to its causes, with an indefinitely widening network of causes, then a complete analysis of forest fires would be impossible.

So, too, with the analysis of influence. Where we wish to bring our inquiry to a halt depends upon our interests. Returning to Figure 3–1 for a moment, are we primarily interested in explaining the consequences [d] of the President's actions or the actions themselves [b] and [c]? If we choose consequences, are we concerned primarily with the role of the President, with the thought that we might shift these decisions to an independent body? Or are we interested primarily in the relationship between the milk producers and the President, with the thought of regulating campaign contributions? Or are we interested in how certain inequalities in resources, skills, and incentives lead to certain decisions with consequences that reinforce the inequalities?

We may wish to focus on still other linkages. For example, if we want to explain why certain decision-makers, such as the President, make the decisions they do, we could examine the effects of:

Their current values, attitudes, expectations, and information

Their earlier or more fundamental attitudes, values, beliefs, ideologies, personality structures, and predispositions

The values, attitudes, expectations, information, beliefs, ideologies, and personalities of others whose actions are in some way relevant to the decision

The process of selection, recruitment, or entry by which decision-makers arrive at their positions

The rules of decision-making they follow, the political structures, the constitutional system

The other institutions of the society—the economic, social, religious, cultural, and educational structures that allocate key resources

The prevailing culture, particularly the political culture

The historical events that influenced the culture, institutions, and structures

And so on.

No doubt a complete explanation of influence relations in a political system would try to describe and explain effects attributable to all these links in the chain of social causation, and others as well. Yet this is such a staggering task that it might well serve as a program for all the social sciences for generations. Meanwhile, it is important to specify the links in the chain one is studying. A good deal of confusion and controversy are produced when analysts focus on different links in the chain of power and causation without clearly specifying what effects they wish to explain. A good deal of criticism of dubious relevance is produced by critics who hold that the investigator has focused on the "wrong" links or did not provide a "complete" explanation. The problem is not that there are two faces of power rather than one, as some writers contend,[20] or even that there are three faces rather than two.[21] The problem is that there are an indefinite number of critical links in the chain of causation and therefore an indefinite number of "faces" of power.[22]

AUTONOMY AND THE PRIME MOVERS

The logical complement of influence is autonomy. To the extent that A influences B on some matter x, then B is not autonomous in relation to A with respect to x. Conversely, B is autonomous in relation to A, with respect to x, to the extent that A does not influence B's actions or intentions with respect to x. If Albert cannot influence Barbara, his supervisor, to grant him an extra week's vacation in the summer, then by definition Barbara is autonomous in relation to Albert with respect to the matter of the vacation. Barbara, of course, may not be autonomous on this matter in relation to actors other than

[20] Peter Bachrach and Morton Baratz, "The Two Faces of Power," *American Political Science Review*, 56 (1962), pp. 947–52.

[21] Steven Lukes, *Power: A Radical View* (London: Macmillan Inc., 1974).

[22] Some of the problems are represented by conflicting interpretations in Steven Rosen, ed., *Testing the Theory of the Military-Industrial Complex* (Boston: D. C. Heath & Co., 1973).

Albert. For example, her decision on Albert's vacation may be completely controlled by Arthur, the general manager.

In an isolated and comparatively small system we might discover actors who are autonomous in relation to all other actors on matters of crucial importance. These would be the "prime movers." They are no doubt what we consider "the center of power," "the ruling group," "the power structure," and so on. But in systems that are not small and isolated, discovering prime movers is difficult and may be impossible. Chains of causation extend indefinitely outward and indefinitely backward in time, to include other actors who influence the actors who influence the actors who . . . ad infinitum. In these cases, the network of causation is an indefinitely expanding universe.

The indefinite expansibility of causal networks poses problems not only for the analysis of influence but also for the analysis of a great many causal systems in nature and society. In practice, whether in political analysis or the natural sciences, the indefinite expansibility of causation can be dealt with only by deliberately specifying the boundaries of the system in which we happen to be interested. It may be enough for us to know that on most matters involving Albert's job, Arthur controls Barbara, who controls Albert. But for other purposes, we shall want to ask: Who controls Arthur on these matters?

Some conflicting interpretations contained in different analyses of power arise because actors or institutions that are interpreted as autonomous and influential vis-à-vis the other actors within a given subsystem may be interpreted as not autonomous and relatively less influential vis-à-vis actors or institutions that might be included in a larger system. This regress in the location of prime movers is most visible within hierarchical political systems such as a military unit, a government bureaucracy, a business firm, or a dictatorship. In systems such as these, low-level officials are autonomous in relation to their subordinates; but in relation to their superiors, they are subordinates. The regress might finally be considered to come to a halt with a set of superiors "at the top." But of course the "top" of a particular hierarchy also may not be completely autonomous: The top military officials may be influenced by the Secretary of Defense, who is influenced by the President, who is influenced by . . . .

Thus government and society in a nation-state are usually far more complex than comparatively simple hierarchical systems like those of military units. Hence the prime movers are much more difficult to identify—if, indeed, they exist at all. According to Marxist theory, in capitalist societies, the capitalist class unilaterally rules over the society. In this sense the class as a whole might be considered the prime mover. But the unilateral dominance of the capitalist class is more a theoretical postulate or hypothesis than a well-verified description of contemporary nonsocialist nation-states with "democratic" governments. According to democratic theory, in democracies the people are the prime movers; but few political analysts would regard this as a satisfactory description of the actual political system of any nation-state. Indeed, in systems that are not strictly hierarchical, but operate instead with many mutual controls, there is no reason to suppose that ultimate prime movers exist.

4

FORMS OF INFLUENCE

Describing the head of his committee, a member of congress said, "I wouldn't use the term *powerful*. I'd say *influential*. There's a difference."[1]

To most of us, like the representative, the terms *influence*, *power*, *authority*, and *control* suggest different meanings. Sometimes the nuances in meaning are subtle, even elusive. Like so much of the language of politics and political analysis, the meaning of these terms is vague, unclear, and ambiguous.

Nevertheless, political analysis would be impoverished if we were compelled to work only with the generic meaning of the term *influence*. Many of the "differences that make a difference" would have to be ignored if political analysis could not distinguish the different forms of influence.

Consider, for example, how differences in meaning become crucially important in these two situations:

> By making me aware of my talent as a musician, my music teacher inspired me to become a composer, and for that I owe her eternal gratitude.
>
> By threatening to kill me with the gun he held to my head, the thief forced me to give him the combination to the safe, and robbed me of my life savings.

[1] Quoted in John Manley, *The Politics of Finance: The House Committee on Ways and Means* (Boston: Little, Brown & Co., 1970), pp. 122–23.

Both are instances of influence in the generic sense of the term. But what a difference!

Although it is important to be able to make distinctions, this does not mean that we can make these distinctions simply by stipulating a number of definitions.[2] The concern of this chapter is meaning—the semantic aspect of analysis. Indeed, because of the necessity to convey meaning in political analysis, works that convey the optimum understanding of power and influence in concrete situations are often detailed, descriptive, subtle, and employ a vocabulary of variety and nuance. In this chapter, attention will be called to forms of influence that make a difference to us. The distinctions will help us to understand influence even if an adequate description of a complex political system, such as a local community, would require discriminating language beyond the concepts in this chapter.

INFLUENCE: POSITIVE AND NEGATIVE

The generic relationship defined in the last chapter is referred to by different names—influence, control, power, and authority. Since the word influence accords moderately well with common usage, I propose to use it as the name for the generic relationship.

We have already seen how "implicit influence" may be distinguished from "manifest influence." In doing so, I refrained from calling attention to one aspect of influence that might seem anomalous. To determine whether A influences B, the concept in the last chapter did not explicitly require that B must respond in a way that is favorable to A's desires.[3] One ordinarily takes this for granted. Sometimes, however, one might want to describe instances of negative influence—that is, where A causes B to respond, but against, rather than in accordance with, A's desires. It has been said, for example, that when a large program of economic aid intended to speed European recovery after World War II was attacked by the Soviet leader, Joseph Stalin, the result was to *increase* Congressional support for the proposal. Most of the time, of course, what interests us is not negative influence of this kind, but positive influence, or *control.*

Forms of control do not have crystalline boundaries. They merge into one another. I can not offer a well-defined point on the continuum at which one form definitely becomes another. There is a problem here, but because it is one that confronts a vast amount of political and social inquiry, I do not

[2] In an appendix to the Italian translation of the first edition of this book, I showed how 14,000 different forms of influence could be defined!

[3] For ease of exposition, I shall continue to refer to only two actors. It should be remembered, however, that influence relationships can involve a multiplicity of actors in complex causal networks, and usually do.

wish to stress it further. The problem is not, certainly, unique to the analysis of influence.

THE MEANS OF INFLUENCE

By definition, A controls B if A's desires cause a change in B's actions or predispositions. Differences in the means by which B's actions or preferences are altered are of crucial significance. Consider again the examples given a moment ago. To help the student realize her potentialities as a composer, the music teacher probably relied very heavily on communicating information that affected the student's perceptions of the alternatives open to her and thus changed her actions or predispositions. The thief, however, relied on changing his victim's perceptions of the alternatives by changing the alternatives themselves: both by presenting the victim with two wholly new alternatives and excluding possibilities previously available, and by making sure that the balance of advantage heavily favored one alternative—yielding the combination of the safe as against the risk of being shot.

Ordinarily, when A actually changes the alternatives available to B, A also will make sure that B perceives the change. If B fails to notice the change, B's understanding of the situation remains unchanged, and the action A desires may not be forthcoming. Sometimes, however, A may affect B's understanding of the situation *only* by communicating information to B. "Look out! That's a live wire!" is likely to be sufficient to affect B's actions if B hasn't noticed the power line blown down by the recent storm. The objective alternatives are unchanged: it is still the case that B can either pay no attention to the power line and run the risk of electrocution or pay attention to it and avoid injury. A has not changed these alternatives. What A has changed is B's perceptions of the alternatives. That change has come about purely by means of A's sudden communication of new and critically important information. In the extreme case, if B already has been trained to respond more or less automatically to specific stimuli—such as a command, order, or request—the aspect of the communication that brings about B's actions is devoid of information about rewards. B simply responds in a way that he or she has learned is appropriate to this particular sign, signal, cue, or stimulus.

In practice, of course, a relationship of influence may depend upon a combination of these different means. Nonetheless, in order to clarify the critical differences among possible means of influence, it is useful to distinguish between means in the following way. Influence through communication that consists of a cue or signal might be called *control by training*. Influence by means of communications that provide information (correct or misleading) about the advantages and disadvantages of alternative courses of action can be called *persuasion*. Influence by means that bring about a change in the nature of the alternatives themselves by adding advantages to an alternative or imposing new disadvantages on an alternative, or both, can be called *inducement.*

Persuasion and inducement are themselves broad categories. Each contains subtypes of such great practical and moral difference that the distinctions have been emphasized since Socrates in all forms of political analysis, no matter whether the emphasis is primarily empirical, normative, policy, or semantic.

Trained Control

A common assumption is that learning comes about (whether exclusively so or not) through reinforcement of particular actions by means of rewards. This view contends that habitual responses are those that have been satisfactorily reinforced in the past. On this assumption, then, trained control is a product of prior persuasion and inducements. Yet once B is trained, then persuasion and inducement become unnecessary, except for occasional reinforcement or retraining.

Because the initial period of training requires persuasions and inducements, trained control is not costless. But once the training is completed, the costs of trained control are ordinarily very low, for they consist of the costs of communicating the necessary cues or signals. Moreover, a large share of the costs of trained control is often borne not by the actor currently exercising control, but by social units such as the family, peers, schools, and previous work organizations.

Because it is impossible to grow up without developing habitual responses, a considerable element of trained control exists in every society. It may be that there is some component of trained control in most enduring relations of influence. It is, certainly, a ubiquitous form of influence.

Persuasion

Rational Persuasion. One form of persuasion that often is singled out as humane and desirable takes place by means of rational communication—a successful effort by A to enable B to come to an understanding of the "true" situation by means of truthful information.[4] Persuasion by rational communication *(rational persuasion)* is consistent with Kant's moral injunction that one should treat other human beings always as ends in themselves, never as means to an end. In this respect, some people might object to conceiving of rational persuasion as influence at all. Yet it is, as a few examples will show.

A physician warns a patient: "If you don't stop smoking three packs of

[4] Akin to rational persuasion is the "ideal speech situation" and the "communicative ethics" described by the German philosopher and social theorist Jurgen Habermas. See his "Towards a Theory of Communicative Competence," *Inquiry*, 13:4 (Winter 1970), pp. 360–75. For a brief account and critique, see William A. Galston, *Justice and the Human Good* (Chicago: University of Chicago Press, 1980), pp. 41–46. For a fuller exposition, see Thomas McCarthy, *The Critical Theory of Jurgen Habermas* (Cambridge: MIT Press, 1979), Chap. 4, pp. 272–357.

cigarettes a day, you run a high risk of lung cancer. And you certainly aren't doing your weak heart any good either." A lawyer advises a client: "My best judgment is that if you take this to court, you'll lose." An architect apologizes: "I'm sorry, but I've costed out the house you had in mind, and it is going to cost you at least twice the figure you stipulated as your outside limit." In each case, if the client responds to the alternatives in the light of this new information, the physician, lawyer, or architect has caused the client to do something that he or she otherwise would not have chosen to do. In terms of influence, the desires of the professional have affected the client's actions or predispositions to act.

It is no accident that the examples I have chosen are all drawn from relations between professionals and clients. A professional code of conduct requires that in relationships with the client, professionals transmit only information that is, to the best of their knowledge, truthful.

Manipulative Persuasion. Rational persuasion represents rational communication in its purest form. But there are many dishonest forms of communication in which there is no intention of transmitting only truthful information. Persuasion can be deliberately deceptive. Here A seeks to persuade B to act not by providing a correct understanding of the alternatives based upon truthful information but by means of manipulating B's understanding. Manipulative persuasion exists when A influences B by communication that intentionally distorts, falsifies, or omits aspects of truth known to A that if made known to B would significantly affect B's decision. Most advertising is a form of manipulative persuasion.

Unlike rational persuasion, manipulative persuasion is inconsistent with Kant's moral imperative: In manipulative persuasion persons are treated not as ends but as means, instruments, or subjects. Although manipulative persuasion usually is thought to occupy a moral standing far beneath rational persuasion, in philosophical and ideological statements great ends are not infrequently held to justify intrinsically bad means. Thus Plato recommended manipulative persuasion in order to establish his ideal Republic.[5] Political movements across the spectrum from Left to Right have followed Plato's footsteps. Former President Nixon and his advisers justified the great Watergate cover-up on these grounds.

Inducement

Often when A wishes to control B with respect to some scope of activity, it is insufficient for A to communicate information—truthful or deceptive—about the alternatives B supposedly confronts. An employer who warns employees, "If you go on strike, you'll lose your wages," ordinarily would be telling the truth, but the employees might nonetheless choose to strike. The

[5] G. M. A. Grube, trans. *Plato's Republic.* (Indianapolis: Basic Books, 1974) lines 414d–415d

employer might try to manipulate employees' understanding by dubious truth or even by outright lies: "Look, if you go on strike, you'll never get another job with this company." Yet the employer might still fail to persuade workers who believe that their wages are too low, and therefore they will join their fellow workers in a strike for higher wages. The employer might prefer to avoid a strike altogether by giving in to a wage raise, thus inducing the employees to stay on the job. The employer influences employees by changing the nature of the alternatives themselves: The employer adds to the attractiveness of remaining on the job in comparison with striking.

In comparison with rational persuasion, which is generally considered a good means of influence, and manipulative persuasion, which is widely condemned (although widely practiced), influence by means of rewards has no definite moral standing one way or another. Nearly everyone, I imagine, considers positive inducements good in some situations and bad in others. To judge whether the employer is right to offer employees higher pay not to strike and whether an employee is right to accept it, would require a thorough analysis of the situation and a social-political perspective, an ideology or a political philosophy, that would provide grounds for arriving at a judgment.

Power. With other kinds of influence by inducements, however, the ethical questions are more acute and direct. Suppose, for example, that an employer says: "A strike is in violation of the company's contract with the union. If you go on strike, I'll get an injunction and within twenty-four hours you'll be in jail." In addition suppose that this is a truthful statement. Whereas in the preceding example the employer changed the employee's preference ordering by adding an alternative consisting of a positive inducement, in this example the employer modifies an existing alternative—to strike—by adding the prospect of severe punishment. Influence of this kind, when compliance is attained by creating the prospect of severe sanctions for noncompliance, is often called power.[6]

Such a conception of power may have been in the minds of members of the Ways and Means Committee who denied that their chairman, Wilbur Mills, exercised "power" over them:

> Power—you mean influence? In the sense of influence? I agree with that. He's considerate. He's as considerate of the most junior member as he is of the most senior. That's why he's "powerful."

[6] This accords with the definition of Harold D. Lasswell and Abraham Kaplan, in *Power and Society* (New Haven: Yale University Press, 1950): "A *decision* is a policy involving severe sanctions (deprivations). . . . *Power* is participation in the making of decisions. . . . It is the threat of sanctions which differentiates power from influence in general. Power is a special case of the exercise of influence: it is the process of affecting policies of others with the help of (actual or threatened) severe deprivations for nonconformity with the policies intended." Lasswell cites as comparable John Locke's use of the term in the *Two Treatises of Government* (1690): "Political Power, then, I take to be a right of making laws, with penalties of death, and consequently all less penalties" pp. 74–76.

> I wouldn't use the term powerful, I'd say influential. There's a difference. I'll compare him with . . . Carl Vinson. Carl had power and he used it, he wasn't afraid to use it. Mills is different. He has influence. I don't mean influence in the sense you peddle influence. It isn't "you do this for me" or on a committee assignment . . . He can always bring you together. He has such great respect and influence.[7]

Exactly what constitutes a "severe" loss or deprivation is somewhat arbitrary. What a person regards as severe varies with experiences, culture, bodily conditions, and so on. Nonetheless, probably among all peoples, exile, imprisonment, and death are considered severe punishments. Therefore, whoever can impose these penalties is bound to be important. Indeed, the State is distinguishable from other political systems only to the extent that it successfully upholds the claim to the exclusive right to determine the conditions under which severe penalties—those involving serious physical pain, constraint, punishment, or death—may be legitimately employed.

Coercion. Suppose that, in a strike situation, Carson, desperately wants to go on working. His wife is ill, he has staggering medical expenses, his unpaid bills are overwhelming, he is about to sell his car and his house to scrape up cash—and the union has no strike fund. In these circumstances, Carson's preferences are, from best to worst:

1. To go on working at the same pay
2. To quit and find another job
3. To strike

But let us suppose that the labor union has been taken over by criminal elements who use the strike weapon to extort protection money from business firms. Allston, a union agent, threatens: "Carson, if you don't go on strike, and you try to go through our picket line, we'll beat you to a pulp. And don't thing you can sneak off and get another job either. Your kids might just have an accident on the way to school. Your're going to join the strike—or else." After thinking it over, Carson now feels that his only alternatives are, from best to worst:

1. To strike
2. To go on working (and be badly beaten up)
3. To quit (and have his children injured)

Carson is caught. From his point of view, his options are all unsatisfactory. He is compelled to do what he had not wanted to do at all because the

[7] Manley, *The Politics of Finance*, pp. 122–23. Manley, it should be said, interprets these remarks as implying a difference between a one-way relationship (power) and a "mutual process of stimulation" (influence).

only remaining alternatives are much worse. If he tried to explain his situation, Carson might say, "I don't want to strike but I *have* to. I have no choice. They're forcing me to do it." In this situation, a philosopher might say that Carson is coerced.

In this instance the relationship involves a particularly sinister form of power because all the options open to Carson entail severe sanctions. No matter what he does, Carson will be a good deal worse off. He is compelled to choose a damaging alternative because all the others are even worse. This is coercion. The classic case of coercion is the one illustrated at the beginning of this chapter: "Your money or your life!"

Just as power is a form of influence, so coercion is a form of power. But not all power is strictly coercive in the sense just defined. If positive inducements are combined with severe sanctions to bring about the action desired, the relationship is one of power but not of coercion in the strict sense.

Physical Force. Power and coercion do not necessarily require the use or threat of physical force. However, physical force, although it is an inefficient form of influence, too clumsy and costly for most purposes, is often involved in power and coercion. Despots may rule by fear, but never only by force. Even a despot needs guards, jailers, and a military that is loyal and obedient. And the despot alone cannot gain obedience from every soldier, jailer, or guard to comply by direct force.

What makes coercion effective is not the actual use of physical force, rather it is the threat to harm another by physical force if the other does not comply. The threat of force often makes coercion an effective goal or deterrent to action. The actual use of force occasionally may help make the threat credible. But if the threat must always be carried out, coercion by force becomes self-defeating. A thief may turn a live victim into a dead one; but a corpse cannot open the safe. If the great powers should ever carry out the threat of nuclear war, there may be no survivors. The actual employment of physical force, then, usually signifies that a policy based on the threat of force has failed.

Unilateral and Reciprocal Control

Control is not necessarily one-way, or unilateral. It may also be mutual, or reciprocal. Consider a discussion in which each person influences the others by rational persuasion. Or imagine a member of congress who always tries to vote on legislation so as to please the constituents back home. Because of the anticipated reactions of this member of congress, the constituents are firmly in control of their representative. But if the representative succeeds in keeping the constituents accurately informed, they may, in turn, be influenced by rational persuasion to vote for the representative at the next election.

Exchanges or transactions, which are as ubiquitous in political as in economic life, appear always to involve mutual control: Each party to an exchange modifies his or her actions in response to the offers or promises of the other.

Perhaps the most consequential contemporary instance of reciprocal control is the system of mutual deterrence that has helped to prevent nuclear war. The leaders of each country make their decisions in anticipation of the probable response of the other country's leaders. Since each set of leaders anticipates their own country's destruction in a nuclear war, each side chooses alternatives that do not involve the use or the immediate threat of using nuclear weapons. While the leaders of the Soviet Union and the United States are autonomous in relation to one another on most decisions they make, on military and diplomatic decisions they are involved in a system of reciprocal control. It is fragile, but of unparalleled importance for survival.

EVALUATING FORMS OF INFLUENCE

These distinctions are important to us because of their moral and practical significance. Most of us tend to regard rational persuasion, for example, as more desirable than coercion. To make a thoughtful evaluation of the different forms of influence is no easy matter. I can do no more here than to offer a few suggestions that ought to be considered an introduction and not a conclusion to the subject.

Among the forms of influence, rational persuasion may have a claim to a unique moral standing. The grounds for such acclaim would be something like this: Because, by definition, the only means it employs is the accurate communication of information believed to be strictly true, rational persuasion is a form of enlightenment. To the extent that the information conveyed by rational persuasion is in fact true, it cannot be intrinsically harmful to the other. It may forecast possible harm: "If you do not stop smoking, you may incur lung cancer." But rational persuasion is itself intrinsically neutral: By itself it neither adds to nor subtracts from the good of the other. It is, however, desirable instrumentally (or extrinsically) because through enlightenment it may bring about the good of the other: Armed with knowledge acquired through rational communication, the other may now choose the better rather than the worse alternative—or, at the least, accept the inevitable.

It is no accident, then, that a notion of mutual influence based on rational persuasion lies often half-hidden in the heart of many conceptions of an ideal society. In the eyes of many Athenians, an ideal polis might well have had this quality. Influence in the assembly by gifted leaders like Pericles would rest solely on their exceptional capacity for rational persuasion.

Rousseau's conception of a republic in which every citizen is morally free and yet bound by laws of his own choosing also partakes of this idea. Citizens engage in mutual, rational persuasion and accept freely the obligations created by the collective decisions taken at the conclusion of the discussion. This is an implicit ideal in a great deal of democratic thought. It is often an even more explicit ideal in anarchist thought.

Yet no large number of persons has ever interacted over an extended period of time in and outside their group without developing means of influence other than rational persuasion.

Manipulative persuasion, power, coercion, the threat and application of physical force are commonplace aspects of political life. Every State uses power internally to secure compliance with the policies of the Government. Manipulative persuasion, power, coercion, and physical force have been common in the relations among States; in international politics, war or the threat of war has frequently been used as an alternative to stalemate or peaceful adjustment. Civil wars and revolutions also involve power and coercion; each side resorts to physical force to impose its will on others. It is easy for people accustomed to relatively stable political systems such as those of Britain and the United States to lose sight of the frequency of revolutions, civil wars, and violence. Even today, in large parts of the world, civil strife, guerrilla warfare, revolutionary struggles, terrorism, violence, and suppression of political opponents by physical force are normal and commonplace political practices. It may help Americans to understand the pervasiveness of "internal war" if they remember that our Civil War lasted five years and was one of the bloodiest exhibitions of fratricide in modern history.

Although these things happen, this is not to say that they are morally justified. One might ask, then, whether anything other than rational persuasion can ever be morally justified. After all, manipulative persuasion violates a fundamental and widespread eithical injunction the favors truth over lying. Power, particularly in the form of coercion and where physical force is employed, involves the prospect of inflicting pain on another person, sometimes even causing death. Thus power may be, and coercion surely is, intrinsically harmful.

To avoid intrinsically undesirable means, one might conclude that the only morally permissible means of influence is rational persuasion. Let me call this the *absolute principle* of rational persuasion. Yet this solution immediately leads to self-contradiction unless it is universally adopted. Suppose that some persons use manipulative persuasion or coercion to get what they want. How are we now to apply the principle of rational persuasion? On the one hand, we might conclude that the principle enjoins us to use only rational persuasion in order to dissuade the violators of that principle. Yet if rational persuasion proves ineffectual, as it will in many cases, then we have no effective way of upholding our principle in practice. Alternatively, then, in order to enforce our principle, we might punish or threaten to punish the violators of that principle. But in this case we ourselves will have violated the principle.

Because of this dilemma, it appears that the absolute principle of rational persuasion never can be upheld until it is always adhered to by everyone. Consequently, even pacifists and advocates of nonviolence are rarely prepared to extend their program to cover all situations. Few pacifists would insist that there be no laws regulating air and water pollution, driving speeds through congested areas, the sale and use of firearms, or the conduct of police or onlookers during a peaceful demonstration; or that such laws should not be enforced; or that enforcement must never involve coercive means, such as fines and imprisonment for law-breakers.

Agreement by rational persuasion for some persons can mean coercion for others. In 1787, the American Constitutional Convention negotiated a peaceful settlement of the issues surrounding the new Constitution. One of the compromises of that convention was the perpetuation of slavery. A decade after slavery was abolished as a by-product of a fearfully destructive Civil War, peaceful compromises among national leaders in Washington permitted the rapid restoration of white supremacy in the South. An opponent of slavery or white supremacy confronted, then, the alternatives of persuading white southerners to abandon their beliefs and practices, a feat that even in retrospect seems impossible; to bring about change in the South by force or the threat of force; or to permit the South to impose a dreadful coercion on its black inhabitants.

If these examples show the difficulty in adhering consistently to a position stating that the use of intrinsically undesirable means of influence is never justifiable, they do not controvert the view that some of the means we believe we must employ are intrinsically bad. They help to show, rather, the tragic dilemma that political beings can face. One may or may not face this dilemma responsibly, but so far no one has discovered a way to avoid it.

A second response to this problem, then, is to hold that an action involving power and even coercion is sometimes better than any available alternative. Thus one may judge coercion to be intrinsically bad yet extrinsically or instrumentally desirable in some circumstances. This tension between the intrinsic undesirability of certain means of influence and their unavoidability as instruments is one of the most poignant and troubling problems in our lives as social and political beings.

A third response, following the logic of the second, is to see whether it is possible to create a political system that would tend to reduce the use of coercion and other undesirable forms of control, and tend to increase the use of more desirable forms. To examine this possibility obviously requires us to consider some basic empirical questions. For example, are political systems really so much alike that the differences can hardly matter to us all that much? Or, as I imagine most of us like to believe, do they differ in some pretty important ways? If they do, how? To take one possibility, how do democratic regimes differ from undemocratic regimes? And what conditions in a country will tend to favor one kind of regime or the other? Finally, to what extent is human nature a limit on various possibilities? To what extent do people vary in the way they behave in political life? In the next four chapters we shall briefly explore these questions.

As we have already seen, however, our interest in different forms of control also reflects a concern for certain values or standards, which I have barely touched on in the last few pages. For example, how, if at all, can we justify a belief that a system based on agreement is better than one based on coercion? Or that democracy is better than dictatorship? Or that people have rights to "life, liberty, and the pursuit of happiness"? And so on. In Chapter 9 we shall see how some recent writers have tried to come to grips with issues like these.

5

SIMILARITIES IN POLITICAL SYSTEMS

There are two extreme but common views about political systems. According to one, political systems never vary in their important aspects. According to the other, they are so plastic they can be molded to suit the heart's desire.

Even if, as is the case with practically all disagreements about politics, some of the differences in these perspectives are purely semantic, at base the conflict is more than a matter of words. Consider, for example, the hypothesis that all political systems are dominated by a ruling class or ruling elite, a view associated with three men whose lives spanned the tumultuous changes in Europe during the last quarter of the nineteenth century and the first quarter of the twentieth. Two were eminent Italians: Vilfredo Pareto (1848–1923) and Gaetano Mosca (1858–1941); the third, who was of German birth, lived much of his life in Italy: Roberto Michels (1876–1936). All three achieved acclaim among social theorists disillusioned with or cynical about democracy. A statement by Mosca seems to catch the essence of their argument:

> Among the constant facts and tendencies that are to be found in all political organisms, one is so obvious that it is apparent to the most casual eye. In all societies—from societies that are very meagerly developed and have barely attained the dawnings of civilization, down to the most advanced and powerful societies—two classes of people appear—a class that rules and a class that is

> ruled. The first class, always the less numerous, performs all political functions, monopolizes power and enjoys the advantages that power brings, whereas the second, the more numerous class, is directed and controlled by the first, in a manner that is now more or less legal, now more less arbitrary and violent, and supplies the first, in appearance at least, with material means of subsistence and with the instrumentalities that are essential to the vitality of the political organism.[1]

At the opposite extreme are naive (but not always youthful) enthusiasts poised on the eve of Utopia's arrival, who proclaim, and may even believe, that when the New Day dawns "politics" will disappear.

Observers disagree about what is persistent in politics and what is open to change, and it would be misleading to suggest that in our present state of knowledge the matter can be firmly settled. Each of the extreme views incorporates some of the truth, but each is also incomplete.

As to the view that politics is infinitely plastic, a multitude of experience —most recently that of newly independent nations—shows that after the sun rises on a new society without politics, by high noon the "old" politics has returned with a vengeance. By some standards the new politics may be better, perhaps very much better, than the old; or it may be worse, perhaps very much worse; but in at least some respects the two will be very much alike.

It is these similarities, these stubborn and until now apparently inescapable regularities, to which I wish to call your attention in this chapter.

A Prior Question: How Many? Just how many political systems are there in the world? No one knows. Given the broad definition of "political system" used here, they must number in the millions. In 1978 there were about 154 independent countries and 63 colonies and territories. In one country, the United States, there were 50 states, 3042 counties, 18,862 muncipalities, 16,822 townships and towns, 15,174 school districts, and 25,962 special districts, not to speak of uncounted business firms, trade unions, families, and voluntary associations.[2]

[1] Mosca, *The Ruling Class (Elementi di Scienza Politica,* 1896), ed. Arthur Livingston (New York: McGraw-Hill Book Co., 1939), p. 50. (Copyright 1939 by McGraw-Hill. Used by permission of McGraw-Hill Book Company.) The hypothesis is also set forth by Pareto in *The Mind and Society* (*Trattato di Sociologia Generale,* 1916), 4 vols. (New York: Harcourt Brace Jovanovich, 1935), in vol. 4, p. 1569, and by Michels, *Political Parties* (1915) (New York: Collier Books, 1962), p. 342 ff. A superb study of Mosca that includes as an appendix the final version of his theory of the ruling class is James H. Meisel, *The Myth of the Ruling Class* (Ann Arbor: University of Michigan Press, 1956). An excellent introduction to Pareto will be found in *Vilfredo Pareto: Sociological Writings,* selected and introduced by S. E. Finer (New York: Holt, Rinehart and Winston, 1966). See also S. E. Finer, "Pareto and Pluto-Democracy: The Retreat to Galapagos," *American Political Science Review,* 62 (June 1968): 440–50. A succinct summary and critique of Michels is John D. May's "Democracy, Organization, Michels," *American Political Science Review,* 59 (June 1965): 417–29.

[2] The figures are from *Status of the World's Nations* (Washington, D.C.: U.S. Government Printing Office, 1978), pp. 18–19 and U.S. Bureau of the Census, *Census of Government 1977,* Vol. 1, No. 1, *Governmental Organizations* (Washington, D.C.: U.S. Government Printing Office, 1979).

Our systematic knowledge extends to only a small portion of the behavior of a tiny number of these systems. Political science advances through the specialized study of particular types of political system. What we are seeking in this chapter, however, are the characteristics of political systems in general, or, at any rate, of systems involving more than a handful of people. Remember: these similarities are not a part of the definition of a political system. They are regularities—empirical regularities, one might say—that one can expect to find in any large political system.

CHARACTERISTICS OF POLITICAL SYSTEMS

Uneven Control of Political Resources.

Control over political resources is distributed unevenly. There are four reasons why this is so.

(1) Some specialization of function exists in every society; in advanced societies specialization is extensive. Specialization of function (the division of labor) creates differences in access to different political resources. A Secretary of State and a member of the Senate Foreign Relations Committee have much more access to information about American foreign policy than do most citizens. An officers' cabal in Bolivia has more opportunity to use the threat of force to gain its ends than does a conspiracy among schoolteachers.

(2) Because of inherited differences, not all people start life with the same access to resources, and those with a head start often increase their lead. Individuals and societies are to some extent prisoners of the past; they never start with a completely clean slate either biologically or socially. Some endowments are biological. Many endowments, such as wealth, social standing, or the level of education and aspiration of one's parents, are not biological, however, but social. Whatever their source, differences in biological and social endowments at birth often multiply into even greater differences in resources among adults. Almost everywhere, for example, opportunities for education are related at least in part to the wealth, social standing, or political position of one's parents.

(3) Differences in biological and social inheritance, together with differences in experiences, all produce differences in the incentives and goals of different people in a society. As a practical matter, it is impossible for any society to provide everyone with a standard set of identical motives and aims, a kind of Do-It-Yourself Conformity Kit. Differences in motivation in turn lead to differences in skills and in resources: Not everyone is equally motivated to go into politics, to become a leader, or to acquire the resources that help the leader gain influence over others.

(4) Finally, some differences in incentives and goals usually are encouraged in societies in order to equip individuals for different specialities. If everyone wanted to be a full-time warrior, who would tend the herds or crops? The circle is complete: Whenever specialization of function is regarded as advantageous, some differences in motivations are also thought to be beneficial. But differences in motivations are likely to lead to differences in resources—for example, to greater military prowess for warriors than for shepherds.

For these four reasons[3] it appears to be impossible to create a society in which political resources would be distributed with perfect equality among adults. However, you must not conclude that there are no important differences in the way political resources are distributed in different societies. For there are differences, and they are important. That is a matter for the next chapter.

The Quest for Political Influence. *Some members of the political system seek to gain influence over the policies, rules, and decisions enforced by the government—i.e., political influence.* People seek political influence not necessarily for its own sake, but because control over the government helps them to achieve one or more of their goals. Control over the government is such a familiar way of furthering one's goals or values that it is hard to imagine a political system in which no one sought power. We know from Ruth Benedict's *Patterns of Culture* that the Zuñi Indians of the Southwest not only made no effort to gain power but even avoided it. As a result, they developed an elaborate ritual for imposing the obligations of office on a reluctant member. But this situation is as rare as General Sherman's famous disclaimer, "If nominated, I shall not run, and if elected I shall not serve."

Once again, by way of warning: Don't leap to the conclusion that everyone who seeks political influence does so simply out of a desire for power as such. Although this conclusion is commonplace, the evidence against it is overwhelming. (We return to this question in Chapter 8.)

Uneven Distribution of Political Influence. *Political influence is distributed unevenly among the members of a political system.* Clearly this proposition is closely related to the first one, which dealt with resources. Because some people have more resources with which they can influence the Government, it is easier for them to gain more influence over the Government if and when they wish to do so. People with more influence over the Government can use their influence to gain control over more political resources.

The existence of unequal political influence has been observed for cen-

[3] For a comprehensive treatment, see Gerhard Lenski, *Power and Privilege* (New York: McGraw-Hill Book Co., 1966), especially Chap. Four.

turies; yet although many observers agree on the fact, they disagree in appraising it, some of them justifying it and others attacking it. The opening book of Aristotle's *Politics* sought to explain and justify the differences in the authority of master and slave, husband and wife, parent and child. Twenty centuries later, in the midst of the Enlightenment, Rousseau sought to explain and to attack inequalities of power in his famous essay, *A Discourse on the Origins of Inequality* (1775). Rousseau traced the origins of inequalities of power to inequalities in property. Inequality in property, he maintained, led in turn to inequalities in other resources. Less than a century after Rousseau, Marx and Engels put forth a similar explanation in the *Communist Manifesto* and a series of revolutionary works that followed. Interest in the origins of political inequality contains unabated to the present day. In 1938 Gunnar Landtman, a Finnish anthropologist, followed Rousseau's path by searching for explanations of inequality in an exhaustive examination of preliterate societies. His book bore a title that suggests both Rousseau and Marx: *The Origin of the Inequality of the Social Classes.* In 1951 an American political scientist, David Truman, observed:

> Writers of the most diverse political views and using the most widely variant methods of observation have called attention to the existence in almost all groups of an active minority—identified by such condemnatory terms as "oligarchy" and "Old Guard" or such approving ones as "public-spirited citizens" and "civic leaders."[4]

Sometimes the proposition that political influence is distributed unequally is confused with Mosca's hypothesis that in every political system there is a ruling class. But the one does not imply the other. We shall come back to this distinction in the next chapter, for the presence or absence of a ruling class is one respect in which political systems differ. It is true, though, that if we call the individuals with the greatest political influence the political leaders, then our third proposition implies that every political system has political leaders. And that is the sense in which we shall use the term "leader" or "political leader" in this book: to refer to those individuals who have the greatest influence in a political system.

The Pursuit and Resolution of Conflicting Aims. *Members of a political system pursue conflicting aims, which are dealt with, among other means, by the government of the political system.* Conflict and consensus are both important aspects of political systems. People who live together never agree about everything, but if they are to continue to live together, they cannot wholly disagree in their aims.

Although political theorists have recognized this duality, some have

[4] David B. Truman, *The Governmental Process* (New York: Alfred A. Knopf, 1951), p. 139.

placed more stress on the one than the other. Some, like Hobbes, have emphasized the propensity of people to conflict with one another; others, like Aristotle and Rousseau, their propensity for agreement and cooperation. Political theorists who, like Hobbes, emphasize the tendency of people to pursue conflicting aims are prone to stress the need for concentrated power and authority, obedience, loyalty, conformity, obligation, duty, and discipline. Theorists who, like Aristotle or Rousseau, emphasize people's immense talent for cooperation are more likely to stress how a political system, and particularly the State, can help human beings to pursue common goals, to win dignity and mutual respect, to share freedom, and to behave responsibly. Extreme views on the likelihood of cooperation and conflict usually are accompanied by exteme views about the State. Extreme fear of civic conflict is characteristic of authoritarian patterns of thought. At the other extreme, philosophical anarchists express exceptional confidence in people's cooperative nature.

The Government does not necessarily intervene every time the aims and acts of different individuals conflict. Conflict is often dealt with by nonpolitical means—by gossip, for example, or sorcery, or aggressive language, or even by isolated outbursts of violence. In many societies some form of personal combat is regarded as a normal way to deal with serious personal disagreements. Fistfights were a common occurrence along the American frontier, and in some places they are commonplace even today.

In complex societies a good deal of conflict is mediated, arbitrated, suppressed, resolved, or handled in some fashion by political systems other than the State. However, when a degree of coercion is required that goes beyond what is possible or permitted to other governments operating in the territorial area of the State, officials of the Government can use their superior power by virtue of the Government's exclusive control over the conditions under which violence may be legitimately employed. Thus the Government steps in whenever the conflict is considered beyond adjustments by nonpolitical means or by governments other than that of the State. In the United States, for example, the Government does not ordinarily intervene in labor disputes. But when prolonged conflicts between a union and management in a major industry such as steel threaten to weaken the economy, the President is likely to intervene.

The Acquisition of Legitimacy. *Leaders in a political system try to ensure that whenever governmental means are used to deal with conflict, the decisions arrived at are widely accepted not solely from fear of violence, punishment, or coercion but also from a belief that it is morally right and proper to do so.* According to one usage of the term, a government is said to be "legitimate" if the people to whom its orders are directed believe that the structure, procedures, acts, decisions, policies, officials, or leaders of government possess the quality of "rightness," propriety, or moral goodness—the right, in short, to make binding rules. Thus, our fourth proposition is equivalent to saying: Leaders in a political system try to endow their actions with legitimacy.

When a leader's influence is clothed with legitimacy, it usually is referred to as authority. Authority, then, is a special kind of influence, legitimate influence. Hence, our fourth proposition is also equivalent to: Leaders in a political system try to convert their influence into authority. Because they often succeed, legitimacy is widespread and important. A writer as far-ranging in his curiosity as Max Weber saw fit to concern himself almost exclusively with legitimate governments and authority, evidently in the belief that power without legitimacy was too rare to be worth studying.

It is easy to see why leaders strive for legitimacy. Authority is a highly efficient form of influence. It is not only more reliable and durable than naked coercion but it also enables a ruler to govern with a minimum of political resources. It would be impossible to rely on fear and terror, for example, to carry out the complex tasks of a large bureaucratic organization such as the U.S. Postal Service, the Department of Defense, Massachusetts General Hospital, General Motors, or the public school system of New York City. Also it probably would be impossible, or at any rate much more costly, to rely simply on direct rewards, for this would require an unwieldy "piece-rate" system. When subordinates regard the orders and assignments they receive as morally binding, only a relatively small expenditure of resources, usually in the form of salaries and wages, is necessary to ensure satisfactory performance.

Although many different kinds of political systems can acquire legitimacy, democracies may be more in need of it than most other systems. In the long run, democracy cannot be forced on a group of people against their will; in fact, democracy is unlikely to survive when a large minority opposes it, for democratic institutions would encounter rough going if a majority always had to impose its rule on a large minority.

An enormous variety of political systems seem to have gained considerable legitimacy in various times and places. Even in the relatively democratic society of the United States, political systems that reflect quite contradictory principles of authority acquire legitimacy. For example, business firms, government agencies, and some religious associations are organized according to hierarchical rather than democratic principles. Yet many citizens who concede legitimacy to the American government because of its democratic structure also concede legitimacy to these hierarchical systems.[5] In some time

[5] However, Harry Eckstein has argued that instability is likely if there is a lack of congruence among different authority structures in the same country. See his *Division and Cohesion in Democracy: A Study of Norway* (Princeton: Princeton University Press, 1966), Appendix B and passim. And "Authority Relations and Governmental Performance: A Theoretical Framework," *Comparative Political Studies*, 2 (October 1969): 283–87.

and place, almost every conceivable political arrangement—feudalism, monarchy, oligarchy, hereditary aristocracy, plutocracy, representative government, direct democracy—has acquired so much legitimacy that people have volunteered their lives in its defense.

Development of an Ideology. *Leaders in a political system usually espouse a set of more or less persistent, integrated doctrines that purport to explain and justify their leadership in the system.* A set of doctrines of this kind is often called a political ideology (Mosca called it a "political formula").[6] One reason why leaders develop an idelogy is obvious: to endow their leadership with legitimacy-to convert their political influence into authority. And it is far more economical to rule by means of authority than by means of coercion.

Some leaders, including the highest governmental officials and their allies, usually espouse an ideology that justifies not only their own leadership but also the political system itself. Their ideology is then the official or reigning ideology. A reigning ideology indicates the moral, religious, factual, and other assumptions that are assumed to justify the system. A highly developed reigning ideology usually contains standards for appraising the organization, policies, and leaders of the system, and also an idealized description of the way in which the system actually works, a version that narrows the gap between reality and the goal prescribed by the ideology.

In the United States, the reigning political ideology is "democracy." To be sure, the depths of the commitment, the extent to which the implications of various tenets in the ideology are understood, and the willingness to apply principles to concrete cases, all vary a great deal among Americans. Whatever the discrepancies between pronouncements and behavior, however, "democracy" is clearly the reigning ideology among Americans.[7]

Despite the fact that a reigning ideology helps incumbent leaders acquire legitimacy, it would be highly unrealistic to conclude that the existence or content of an ideology can be completely explained by the desires of leaders to clothe their actions with legitimacy and thus to transform naked power into authority. For one thing, the fact that many people who are not leaders accept the ideology reflects a desire for explanation, an interpretation of experiences and goals, that offers meaning and purpose to life and to one's place in the universe. It would be surprising if people, who for thousands of years sought to comprehend the relative motions of planets and stars did not also want to understand their own political order. Thus illiterate peasants living in conditions of great physical and psychological deprivation frequently

[6] Mosca, *The Ruling Class*, pp. 70–71.

[7] For some comparisons, see Jack Dennis, Leon Lindberg, Donald McCrone, and Rodney Stiefbold, "Political Socialization to Democratic Orientations in Four Western Systems," *Comparative Political Studies*, 1 (April 1968): 71–101.

adopt an outlook on the world that "explains" and justifies their inequality, suffering, and frustrations.[8]

Moreover, despite appearances to the contrary, leaders cannot arbitrarily invent and manipulate a reigning ideology, for once a political ideology is widely accepted in a political system, the leaders, too, become its prisoners. They run the risk of undermining their own legitimacy if they violate its norms.

They may even find it impossible to carry out their policies. For example, in 1936 President Roosevelt was reelected by an enormous majority. When the Supreme Court declared one key New Deal measure after another unconstitutional, he resolved to overcome the hostile majority on the Court by obtaining from Congress permission to appoint six new members. But he evidently did not anticipate the resentment that such an attempt to "pack" the Court would generate, even among the people who voted for him and supported his policies. In the fall of 1936 and the winter of 1937, a sizable majority of people evidently felt that the Supreme Court should be "more liberal in reviewing New Deal measures." Yet when the President unveiled his startling proposal in February 1937, it was at once opposed by a substantial majority in Congress and a small majority among the general public. As the debate wore on, the magnitude of the opposition both in Congress and in the country increased. By June, surveys indicated that 60 percent of the people interviewed did not want Congress to pass the legislation.[9] In July the bill was killed. Roosevelt never regained the influence he had once enjoyed over Congress on domestic matters. Indeed, during the struggle over the Court, Roosevelt's northern Republican and southern Democratic critics in Congress learned how to form a coalition against the President, and this lesson they never forgot.

It would be unrealistic, however, to assume that a reigning ideology is a unified, consistent body of beliefs accepted by everyone in a political system. In the first place, the extent to which a distinguishable ideology is actually developed and articulated varies enormously from one political system to another. Many political systems simply share the reigning ideology that lends legitimacy to the Government and the State. Thus it would be a good deal more difficult to specify the prevailing ideology among members of the United Automobile Workers or General Motors than among Americans generally. In the second place, no ideology is ever entirely integrated or internally consistent. For one thing, an ideology is not necessarily static: New

[8] Mehmet Bequiraz, *Peasantry in Revolution* (Ithaca, N.Y.: Center for International Studies, Cornell University, 1966).

[9] For survey data, see Hadley Cantril, ed., *Public Opinion, 1935–1946* (Princeton: Princeton University Press, 1951), pp. 149–51, 755–57. For Roosevelt's proposal and strategy, see Joseph Alsop and Turner Catledge, *The 168 Days* (Garden City N.Y.: Doubleday & Co., Inc., 1938).

situations create a need for new explanations and emphasis on new goals, and thus novel and unrelated or even inconsistent elements creep in. Then, too, a certain amount of ambiguity is sometimes a positive advantage precisely because it permits flexibility and change. The fact that the Soviet ideology is ambiguous about how and when the final condition of full communism is to be reached permits Soviet leaders more free play than they would have if it prescribed a rigid timetable of specific steps.

Third, a reigning ideology is probably never uniformly accepted by all members of a system. Many members have only rudimentary knowledge of the prevailing ideology articulated by the leaders; others may actually hold—perhaps unwittingly—a variety of private views that are at odds with the reigning ideology. For all his insight and remarkably acute observations, Tocqueville no doubt exaggerated the uniformity with which Americans subscribed to democratic ideals in the 1830s. Certainly there is great variation among Americans today. Citizens who agree that opponents should have the right to criticize the government disagree on the rights of Communists or revolutionaries to advocate changes. People who profess to believe in free speech may nonetheless favor the suppression of dissent. Moreover, for many people the reigning ideology, or any ideology at all, is too remote, too unimportant, too abstract, or too complex to grasp except in highly rudimentary form.

Fourth, the reigning ideology may be rejected. Some members of a political system—communists or fascists in a democratic country, or democrats in an authoritarian country—may adhere to rival and conflicting ideologies. Because people differ in their aims, incumbent leaders rarely rule without incurring opposition, overt or covert; few systems can count on ungrudging support from all their members. Opponents of a regime often formulate criticism that denies the existing system its legitimacy. Often, too, critics depict an alternative that, unlike their portrayal of the existing system, is held to repose on a legitimate foundation.

Sometimes the revolutionary ideology of one period becomes the reigning ideology of the next. In the eighteenth century, democratic doctrine was revolutionary ideology; today, it is the reigning ideology in the United States and most of western Europe. In Russia, Marxism and Leninism were revolutionary ideologies until 1917; since then they have become reigning ideologies modified by Lenin's successors.

Since ideologies seem to rise and fall, and the reigning ideology of one system contradicts that of another, does one ideology possess just as much factual and moral validity as another? To anyone who finds the burden of choosing among conflicting views excessive, this view is seductive. But for good or ill, political appraisal is not easy. Nothing that has been said—and nothing that will be said later—supports the notion that all ideologies are equally valid. We return to this issue in Chapter 9.

The Impact of Other Political Systems. *The way a political system behaves is influenced by the existence of other political systems.* With occasional exceptions so rare that they can be ignored—a small and completely isolated club or tribe, for example—political systems do not exist in isolation.

Exceptional cases aside, every political system engages in foreign relations, for the actions open to one system are affected by the past or probable actions of others. A city cannot successfully ignore the existence of a national government; national governments must adapt their actions to the hard fact that other national governments, alliances, coalitions, and international organizations also exist. Even a club or a religious congregation cannot act with complete autonomy; and the leaders of a trade union must take into account the past or probable actions of business firms, other unions, and the government.

It is a curious fact that most people who portray their vision of an ideal political system ignore the limits imposed by the existence of other political systems. It is easy to imagine "the good society" if one does not bother with other, and quite possibly bad, societies that might clutter up the surrounding landscape. Consequently, political Utopias are usually portrayed without the troublesome limitations imposed by foreign relations, which are eliminated by either ignoring them entirely or solving them according to some simple plan.

In this respect the influence of Greek thought has been pernicious, for the emphasis of Greek political theorists on the virtues of a small, autonomous, self-sufficient State and their assumption that war was the natural and inevitable relation among States led them to ignore the usual problems of foreign affairs when States were not at war. In all Plato's Dialogues, which have had an enormous impact on Western political thought, there are only a handful of references to foreign affairs. Aristotle criticized Plato for the omission. "If a polis," he wrote in *The Politics*, "is to live in a political life [involving intercourse with other states] and not a life of isolation, it is a good thing that its legislator should also pay regard to neighboring countries."[10] Yet Aristotle had little more to say about foreign relations than Plato. By contrast, in modern times the study of foreign relations has developed into a special branch of political science.[11]

But how can we distinguish foreign relations from internal politics? How, in other words, can we distinguish one political system from another? What are the "boundaries" of a political system? Fortunately, boundaries often are assigned to a political system by convention. Conventional boundaries may be geographical, in which case everyone within the geographical boundaries is considered to be "in" (even if not always "of") that particular

[10] Ernest Barker, ed., *The Politics of Aristotle* (Oxford: Oxford University Press, 1952), p. 57. Words in brackets interpolated by the editor, Ernest Barker.

[11] The subject is treated in Karl Deutsch's *Analysis of International Relations*, 2nd ed. (Englewood Cliffs, N.J.: Prentice-Hall, Inc., 1978).

system. Or membership may depend on some such conventional characteristic as paying dues, earning wages, or simply being listed as a member or employee. Because of the existence of understandings like these, it is easy to agree on the conventional boundaries of the United States, California, the U.S. Senate, the Supreme Court, the House of Representatives, the AFL-CIO, and the Benevolent and Protective Order of Elks.

Do boundaries of this kind rest on anything more than convention? Do they share a more general or abstract property? They do, and in political analysis we often employ this property to determine whether the conventional boundaries coincide with the "real boundaries. For example, the People's Republic of China claims that its boundaries include Taiwan. Some Chinese leaders on Taiwan claim, in effect, that their boundaries include the mainland. Now, these moral, legal, or propagandistic claims would not necessarily be altered one iota by abstract political analysis. But it is possible to determine the boundaries of the political system that centers on Taiwan for purposes of analysis regardless of whether these "analytical" boundaries are proper according to legal or moral criteria. In Chapter 1 we defined a political system as any persistent pattern of human relationships that significantly involves power, rule, or authority. Hence, for purposes of political analysis, a boundary can be assigned to a political system wherever there exists a sharp decline in the power of the government of the system to influence action.

The reason why the 2500-mile border between Canada and the United States is not merely a conventional line on a map but a meaningful boundary between two political systems is that the relative power of officials of the American and Canadian governments over one's actions depends very strongly on exactly which side of the border one happens to be on.

There may be many dips in the curve of power of a government; if so, many different points might be regarded as the boundaries of a political system. Which set of points a person uses to bound a system depends on the particular question under analysis. For example, "unlike many European parties, the major American parties have no formal membership procedures, or initiation ceremonies; there are no card-carrying Republicans or Democrats. Yet . . . a large majority of the electorate . . . identifies with one or the other of the major parties."[12] Depending on the problem at hand, political scientists stipulate different boundaries for the parties: The "party" may include only the leaders or activists, for example, or all registered adherents, or, for some purposes, even all party " identifiers."

One should not be disturbed if the boundaries of political systems are somewhat rubbery, for in practice, conventional boundaries are usually sufficient. When they are not, a little attention to the problem one is trying to

[12] Fred I. Greenstein, *The American Party System and the American People*, 2nd ed. (Englewood Cliffs, N.J.: Prentice-Hall, Inc., 1970).

analyze, and some familiarity with the particular system, will usually indicate a number of satisfactory points one can use to trace the bounds.

The Inevitability of Change. It is appropriate to close this chapter by emphasizing a regularity that anticipates the subject of the next: *All political systems undergo change.*

From time immemorial political observers have pointed out the mutability of political systems. "Seeing that everything which has a beginning has also an end," wrote Plato, "even a constitution such as yours will not last forever, but will in time be dissolved." With his characteristic preference for imaginative and somewhat rigid theoretical notions drawn from brilliant speculation but not tested against concrete experience, Plato went on to describe the inevitable process of decay through which even the perfect aristocracy he proposed must degenerate into a "timocracy," or government of honor, to be followed by oligarchy, thence by democracy, and finally by tyranny.

Aristotle rejected Plato's dialectic, but he devoted a lengthy section of *The Politics* to the causes of revolutions and constitutional change; he extended the theory of political change well beyond where Plato had taken it. Because of their solid good sense, his remarks are still worth reading.

Although students of politics have observed the mutability of political sytems, it is an interesting fact that those who set out to reveal the lineaments of an ideal State generally eliminate all change from their Utopia. Being perfect, the ideal State either cannot change or, if it changes at all, must change for the worse. Consequently, political Utopias exclude or deprecate the idea of change. Plato assumed that even his perfect State would change—but that it must inevitably decay into increasingly degenerate forms. (As Aristotle testily pointed out, "When it comes to tyrannies, Plato stops: He never explains whether they do, or do not, change, nor, if they do, why they do so, or into what constitution they change.") Karl Marx turned Plato around. Marx portrayed the whole of history as ceaseless and ineluctable change. Yet once the final state of communism was reached, all the historical forces that had hitherto made for change were, presumably, to vanish. Even democrats sometimes imply that democracy is a final stage in humanity's political evolution. Yet in the entire history of political institutions, no political system has ever been immutable.

Because of the obvious and extraordinary importance of political change, whether peaceful or violent, evolutionary or revolutionary, many attempts have been made to understand it, explain it, and even predict it, to identify different types of change, the conditions that produce them, the sequences or stages through which changes proceed, and so on. Revolutions in particular have generated an enormous amount of investigation and theory. Yet we still lack a systematic understanding of political change or a satisfactory theory about revolution, and our capacity for predicting crucial political changes is still quite poor. Nonetheless, at least two predictions can be made with considerable confidence: (1) In every political system, no matter how solid it may be or appear to be, significant changes are bound to take place; and (2) because change is so difficult to predict, a very large measure of uncertainty is an inescapable feature of political life.

6

DIFFERENCES IN POLITICAL SYSTEMS

The fact that there are regularities among political systems hints that there are limits to change. That political systems differ argues that there are opportunities for change. If the similarities constrain us in what we can do, the differences enlarge the boundaries of what we may reasonably hope to do. Just as an awareness of the regularities may be both depressing and reassuring, so an awareness of the differences may engender hopes—and fears—about politics.

Yet if we have to live in some kind of political system, we do not all have to live in the same kind. It is the real or presumed differences in systems that make one precious, another tolerable, a third hateful.

As with people, so with political systems: Differences are beyond our capacity to enumerate. Political systems have different proportions of people within their boundaries who are red-haired, green-eyed, over five feet tall, under twenty-four hours or over ninety years old, or whose last names begin with the sound "zee."

On Inundation by Data. If all facts are treated equally, we shall soon be inundated by data. For many centuries, information relating to political systems was not only selective but also scarce and impressionistic. Aristotle's feat of collecting information on the "constitutions" or political life of 158

Greek city-states was unique; and even that information was soon lost to posterity. Yet after centuries of wholly inadequate data, in the last few years the amount of information about different political systems has begun to rise at a staggering rate.

The rapidly increased attention to all parts of the world since the Second World War, the growth in global communications, the diffusion throughout the world of political science and other social sciences as fields of active study, the development of data archives, and the increasing demand by political scientists for better data have all contributed to an information explosion in the study of politics.

During the 1960s, for example, whole new collections of data were made available on national political systems, to say nothing of the plethora of studies of subnational and international systems. These included handbooks of quantitative data,[1] classification of countries based on both quantitative and qualitative indicators,[2] analyses of specific problems using data on fifty to a hundred countries,[3] analyses of the results of opinion surveys among a smaller number of countries,[4] and in-depth comparative studies of national political systems of components of national political systems such as political parties or political cultures.[5]

Although this flood of information gives rise to formidable problems of data analysis, it also opens up new and barely exploited opportunities for increasing our understanding of the similarities and differences among political systems, explaining how these come about, and determining their conse-

[1] The most extensive array of carefully prepared cross-national data is contained in the various editions of *World Handbook of Political and Social Indicators.* The second edition by Charles Lewis Taylor and Michael C. Hudson (New Haven: Yale University Press, 1972) contained data on nearly 150 variables for 136 countries. Through the generosity of the authors, in this and later chapters I have been able to draw on data for the third edition by Charles Lewis Taylor and David A. Jodice, *World Handbook of Political and Social Indicators, Third Edition, Vol. 1: Cross National Attributes and Rates of Change* and *Vol. 2: Political Protest and Government Change* (New Haven: Yale University Press, 1983). I want to express my appreciation to the authors for allowing me to make use of their data in advance of the publication of the third edition.

[2] Classification of 115 countries based on both quantitative and qualitative data can be found in Arthur S. Banks and Robert B. Textor, *A Cross-Polity Survey* (Cambridge, Mass.: The M.I.T. Press, 1963).

[3] See, for example, the analysis of the interaction of political, social, and economic factors in 74 countries that were "underdeveloped" as of 1950, in Irma Adelman and Cynthia Taft Morris, *Society, Politics, and Economic Development* (Baltimore: Johns Hopkins Press, 1967).

[4] The pioneering work is Gabriel A. Almond and Sydney Verba, *The Civic Culture* (Princeton N.J.: Princeton University Press, 1963), which compares attitudes in the United States, Britain, Germany, Italy, and Mexico. For another example, see Hadley Cantril, *The Pattern of Human Concerns* (New Brunswick: Rutgers University Press, 1965), based on a special survey of 13 countries.

[5] Notably the seven-volume series on Political Development sponsored by the Committee on Comparative Politics of the Social Science Research Council, and published by the Princeton University Press. For example, the sixth volume, edited by Joseph LaPalombara and Myron Weiner, *Political Parties and Political Development* (1966), contains essays on party systems in most regions of the world except the one-party communist areas.

quences.[6] Considered in this light, modern political analysis is poised at the threshold of a new stage of knowledge.

The Flood of Typologies. The information explosion also has been accompanied by a flood of "typologies," or proposed ways of classifying political systems. In fact, "typology" became such an "in" word among political scientists in the 1960s that it crowded out older but equally usable terms like "classification" or "classification-scheme." At the Seventh World Congress of the International Political Science Association in 1967, entire sessions were devoted to the topic "Typologies of Political Systems."

Schemes for classifying political systems are, of course, as old as the study of politics itself. Aristotle, for example, produced a classification based on two criteria: the relative number of citizens entitled to rule, whether one, few, or many; and whether the rulers governed in "the common interest" or in their own selfish interests.[7] This famous sixfold classification (Table 6–1) has influenced thinking ever since. But a half-century ago, Max Weber offered a classification that has had more influence among later social scientists than Aristotle's. Weber restricted his attention to systems in which the government was accepted as legitimate, and he suggested that the leaders of a political system might claim legitimacy for their rule, and members might accept their claims, on three grounds:

(1) *Tradition:* Legitimacy rests "on an established belief in the sanctity of immemorial traditions" and on the need to obey leaders who exercise the authority according to the traditions. Weber held that this was "the most universal and primitive case" of authority.

(2) *Exceptional Personal Qualities:* Legitimacy is based on "devotion to the specific and exceptional sanctity, heroism, or exemplary character of an individual person" and the moral or political order he or she has revealed or ordained.

TABLE 6–1 Aristotle's Classification

NO. CITIZENS ENTITLED TO RULE	RULERS RULE IN INTEREST OF: ALL	THEMSELVES
One	Kingship (monarchy)	Tyranny
Few	Aristocracy	Oligarchy
Many	Polity	Democracy

[6] See Richard L. Merritt and Stein Rokkan, eds., *Comparing Nations: The Use of Quantitative Data in Cross-National Research* (New Haven: Yale University Press, 1966).

[7] Ernest Barker, ed., *The Politics of Aristotle* (Oxford: Oxford University Press, 1952), Book 3, Chaps. Six and Eight, esp. pp. 110–14. Notice, however, that Aristotle later reveals a more complex scheme by equating oligarchy with rule by the rich and democracy with rule by the poor. See p. 116.

(3) *Legality:* Legitimacy rests on a belief that power is wielded in a way that is legal; the constitutional rules, the laws, and the powers of officials are accepted as binding because they are legal; what is done legally is regarded as legitimate.[8]

To each of these three main grounds for legitimacy, then, there corresponds a "pure" form of authority: (1) traditional authority, (2) charismatic authority (from a Greek word used by early Christians meaning "the gift of grace"), and (3) legal authority.

Weber recognized that these pure forms were abstractions or, as he called them, "ideal types." In an actual political system one might encounter all three kinds of legitimate authority.

Weber's and Aristotle's schemes have been all but pushed aside by the typologies that have crowded into political analysis in recent years.[9] Scholars have suggested that political systems can be fruitfully classified as autocratic, republican, or totalitarian;[10] as mobilization, theocratic, bureaucratic, or reconciliation systems;[11] as modernizing, totalitarian, traditional, and traditionalistic oligarchies plus tutelary and political democracies;[12] as Anglo-American, Continental European, preindustrial or partially industrial, and totalitarian;[13] and as primitive political systems, patrimonial empires, nomad or conquest empires, city-states, feudal systems, centralized historical bureaucratic empires, and modern societies (democratic, autocratic, totalitarian, and "underdeveloped").[14] Two scholars who applied the statistical technique known as factor analysis to sixty-eight characteristics of 115 countries "inductively derived" a typology of eight types of political systems.[15] One scholar swept conventional language into the trashcan by suggesting that political systems can be classified as fused, prismatic, or refracted.[16]

[8] Max Weber, *The Theory of Social and Economic Organization*, trans. A. M. Henderson and Talcott Parsons (New York: Oxford University Press, 1947), p. 328.

[9] Some of these, particularly those relevant to democratic systems, are summarized in Arend Lijphart, "Typologies of Democratic Systems," *Comparative Political Studies*, 1 (April 1968): 3–44.

[10] Bernard Crick, "The Elementary Types of Government," *Government and Opposition* 3 (Winter 1968): 3–20.

[11] David E. Apter, *Choice and the Politics of Allocation* (New Haven: Yale University Press, 1971), pp. 30ff. See also his "Why Political Systems Change," *Government and Opposition*, 3 (Autumn 1968): 411–17, and *The Politics of Modernization* (Chicago: University of Chicago Press, 1965), pp. 22–38.

[12] Edward Shils, "Political Development in the New States," *Comparative Studies in Society and History*, 2 (July 1960): 382–406.

[13] Gabriel A. Almond, "Comparative Political Systems," *Journal of Politics* 18 (August 1956): 391–409.

[14] S. N. Eisenstadt, *The Political Systems of Empires* (New York: The Free Press, 1963), pp. 10–12.

[15] Phillip M. Gregg and Arthur S. Banks, "Dimensions of Political Systems: Factor Analysis of A Cross Polity Survey," *American Political Science Review* 59 (September 1965): 602–14.

[16] Fred W. Riggs, *The Ecology of Public Administration* (Bombay: Asia Publishing House, 1961), pp. 93–97.

After the flood. *Is there one best typology?* Obviously, no. There are thousands of criteria for classifying political systems. Which ones we find most useful will depend on the aspects of politics in which we are most interested. A geographer might distinguish political systems according to the area they occupy, a demographer by the number of persons who are members, a lawyer according to their legal codes. A philosopher or theologian interested in distinguishing "the best" political system will use ethical or religious criteria. A social scientist interested in determining how revolution is related to economic conditions might classify systems by relative income and frequency of revolutions. Just as there is no one best way of classifying people, so too there is no single way of distinguishing and classifying political systems superior to others for all purposes.

Differences that make a difference. If there are innumerable differences between political systems, some are associated with such a broad range of important consequences—particularly consequences for popular government—that they are particularly worth stressing. These are (1) paths to the present, (2) the socioeconomic "level" or degree of "modernity", (3) distribution of political resources and skills, (4) bases of cleavage and cohesion, (5) the magnitude or severity of conflicts, and (6) institutions for sharing and exercising power.

Although in some degree these differences apply to political systems of all sorts, let us focus the discussion by assuming as our frame of reference the political system of a country.

PATHS TO THE PRESENT

Every political system has had, in some respects, a unique past. This is more than an abstract point, for the inheritance of the past bears heavily on the present and influences the future. Differences in their past mean that the countries of the world do not have exactly the same options. A people that has known nothing but centuries of authoritarian rule is not likely to turn into a stable democracy in a week. And as we shall see in a moment, a country's particular path to the present often makes an all but ineradicable imprint on its conflicts, so powerful that internal peace and stability cannot possibly be brought about by a few months of negotiations.

DEGREE OF "MODERNITY"

History leaves political systems embedded in societies that are at different stages of "development" or "modernization." These terms, now widely used among political scientists, have a parochial air about them, but their meaning can be made quite specific—enough so, indeed, to allow for measurement. There are, in short, profound differences from one country to another in the amount of income per capita, literacy, education, technical skills, technology, industrialization, urbanization, newspaper and magazine circulation, electronic communications, transportation facilities, and the like. These all tend to be intercorrelated: A country relatively low (less "developed") in one respect will very likely be relatively low in other respects, and the converse is true as well.[17]

In Table 6–2, 141 countries are divided into five levels of development according to GNP per capita. As the table shows, the higher a country's GNP, the greater the percentage of urban population, literacy, students in higher education, physicians, radios, and voting.

DISTRIBUTION OF POLITICAL RESOURCES AND SKILLS

Political resources and skills are distributed in different ways in different political systems. Although they are distributed unequally in all systems, the degree of inequality varies from one system to the next. For example, knowledge is a political resource that contributes to the formation of political skills. Access to knowledge through literacy and education is distributed unequally; but in some countries the inequality is greater than in others. At one extreme (Angola, Mauritania, Niger, and Mozambique) 97 percent or more of the population aged fifteen and over was illiterate in the mid-1960s. The median for 130 countries was 60 percent literacy. Among the lowest one-tenth of the countries, primary and secondary school pupils do not amount to more than 15 percent of the population between the ages of five and nineteen; among the highest tenth, the figure is over 90 percent.[18]

In all countries, only a minority of the population received a higher education. But at one extreme, in a half-dozen African countries, not more than 5 persons in every 100,000 were enrolled in institutions of higher education, compared, at the other extreme, with the United States (2840), New Zealand (2100) and the Soviet Union (1674). Even among the twenty countries with the largest GNP per capita there were great variations.[19]

Wealth is a political resource, and everywhere wealth is distributed unequally; but the degree of inequality varies. For example, the distribution

[17] See Bruce M. Russett, et al., *World Handbook of Political and Social Indicators* (New Haven: Yale University Press, 1964).

[18] The data in this section are from Taylor and Hudson, *World Handbook*, Tables 4.3 and 4.5.

[19] *Ibid.*, Table 4.4 and 5.5. The figures overstate the differences, since in smaller or poorer countries unable to support institutions of higher education, some people are educated abroad.

TABLE 6-2 Five Levels of Socioeconomic Development—141 countries, 1980

LEVEL	NUMBER OF COUNTRIES (N-141)	GNP PER CAPITA (1978)	% URBAN	% LITERATE	NUMBER OF STUDENTS IN HIGHER EDUCATION PER MILLION	NUMBER OF PHYSICIANS PER MILLION	RADIOS PER THOUSAND
		MEDIAN	MEDIAN	MEDIAN	MEDIAN	MEDIAN	MEDIAN
I	18	$ 155	5%	19%	281	27	21
II	26	$ 260	8%	12%	860	69	37
III	45	$ 680	17%	60%	3,536	277	91
IV	37	$ 2,850	24%	87%	14,610	1205	262
V	15	$10,035	31%	99%	18,123	1705	340

Note: Because of the distorting effects of oil income, OPEC countries are omitted from the table.

Source: Charles Lewis Taylor and David A. Jodice, *World Handbook of Political and Social Indicators, Third Edition, Vol. 1: Cross National Attributes and Rates of Change* (New Haven: Yale University Press, 1983). Reprinted by permission of Yale University Press.

of land, an important form of wealth in agricultural countries, is markedly unequal in all countries. But the inequality in landholdings was considerably more extreme in Iraq, where half the total acreage was occupied by 0.7 percent of the farms, than in Denmark, where half the acreage was taken up by 21 percent of the farms. (See Figure 6–1.)

The extent to which inequalities are correlated also varies from society to society. Suppose every person in a political system were ranked according to relative standing with respect to the most important political resources in that society: let us say wealth, income, knowledge, popularity, control over communications, and command over police and military forces. If everyone's relative standing were the same, thus resulting in a perfect correlation, inequalities in resources would be completely cumulative. The more of one resource an individual had, the more that individual would have of the rest. If, however, an individual's standing on one ranking bore no relationship to other rankings (there is no correlation), inequalities in resources would be dispersed. Dispersion does not mean equality: In a system with completely dispersed inequalities, there could be inequality with respect to every political resource. Nonetheless, the difference between cumulative and dispersed inequalities is a crucial one, for in a society of dispersed inequalities, people lacking one resource might make up for it by having greater control over other resources.

Neither type exists in pure form. There is a strong tendency toward cumulative inequality, yet there appear to be significant differences in the inequalities among political systems. In countries still remaining at one of the

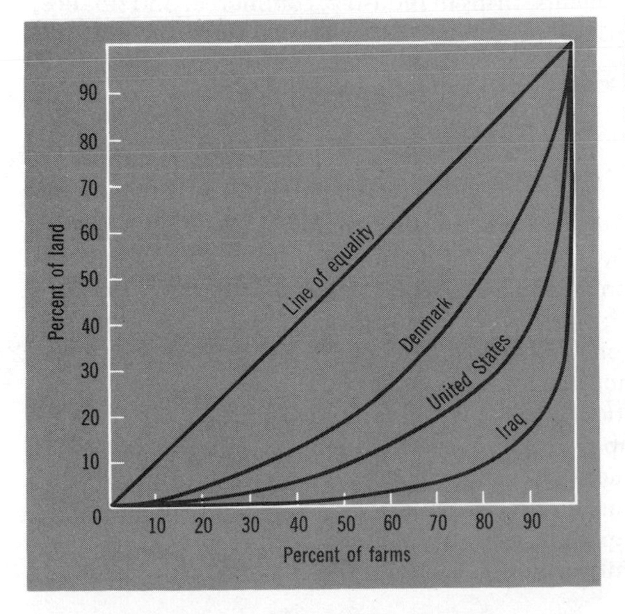

FIGURE 6–1
Lorenz Curve of Land Distribution

Source: Taylor and Hudson, World Handbook, Table 4.14, pp. 267–68.

first three levels in Table 6.2, inequalities are usually highly cumulative. In the Industrial Revolution societies, however, wealth and income shift away from an older feudal aristocracy or landed oligarchy toward the new leaders —in industry, banking, and commerce. Yet for the bulk of the population, in spite of rising incomes, inequalities are still strongly cumulative. (This is the stage that Marx witnessed in western Europe in the mid-nineteenth century.) In the later stages of industrialization, as incomes and mass-consumption continue to increase, there is a further diffusion of technology, literacy, education, affluence, and mass communication. This diffusion also may be accompanied by a marked expansion in interest-group organizations, political skills, and the suffrage. Even in these circumstances inequalities in political resources still persist, but they become less cumulative and more dispersed. Hence it becomes difficult to identify a small, well-defined elite that "runs the country," for different elites tend to exercise influence over different scopes of activity and their relations become highly complex. For example, information and knowledge become unusually important resources for gaining and maintaining influence, and various "information and knowledge elites" come to play crucial roles in decisions. The influence of a president's national security advisor, a Senator's administrative assistant, the staff of a Congressional committee, and the director of Central Intelligence requires skill in receiving, interpreting, shaping, and transmitting crucial, important information often highly specialized and technical, to other key decision makers. But it is not only at these high levels that the need for information enables specialists to acquire influence on decisions; more and more, decision makers within all the institutions of a modern society depend on them, whether local governments, firms in industry, commerce, and finance, trade unions, political parties, or international organizations.

CLEAVAGE AND COHESION

The patterns of political disagreement, conflict, and coalition have different causes in different systems. This proposition and the following paragraphs should be read with caution: It opposes a widespread view that political conflict can be explained by a single source of cleavage, usually an economic characteristic like "class" or "property."

In spite of an enormous amount of speculation, theory, and research, our understanding of political conflict is still limited. Single-factor explanations simply do not stand up well against the data now available. The kinds of individual and group characteristics that are associated with political conflict in countries include not only differences in social status, economic class, income, wealth, and occupation, but also in education, ideology, religion, language, region, and family origins. This multiplicity of factors creates different patterns of political cleavage and cohesion from one country to another.

In the first place, history has left countries with different legacies of characteristics that foster cleavages and cohesiveness, such as language. Because of our experience, Americans may be accustomed to believing that other countries have only one language, which many do; yet our neighbor, Canada, has two. Or compare the Low Countries: The Netherlands has a single language, yet in neighboring Belgium a linguistic boundary has existed for over a thousand years that runs across modern Belgium and divides Walloons, who speak French, from Flemings who speak Flemish, a Germanic language. In Switzerland the boundary between the French- and German-speaking zones has barely changed since it first evolved in the fifth century A.D. On the other side of the world the Indians have over 15 major languages and 500 minor languages and dialects. In fact, in India many minority languages—English is one—are spoken by more people than there are in all of Sweden.[20]

In the second place, history has left varying memories of the past treatment of these differences. Take racial differences. In the United States the enslavement of people of African origin created a castelike system of discrimination that survived long after the abolition of slavery, continues with diminishing force to the present day, and has been the source of severe conflict. By contrast, in Brazil, where an even higher proportion of the population were of African origin and where slavery was not fully abolished until a generation after the American Civil War, the dominant population, which was mainly of Portuguese origin, accepted racial intermixing much more readily. Because of this, even though some racial discrimination exists in Brazil, unlike in the United States, in Brazil it has not been a major source of conflict. Or consider language again. The Swiss nation was built upon equality among its languages; as a result, political conflicts and resentments caused by linguistic differences are nearly negligible. In Belgium, on the other hand, after a flourishing period of Flemish prosperity and preeminence (its brilliance is reflected in the great Flemish painters of the time), an economic and cultural decline led to the subordination of the Flemish to the Walloons, a condition that embittered Belgian politics. In recent years, the economic decline of the Flemish areas has been reversed, while the Walloon region has declined, leading to resentment among the Walloons. Or take religion. In the United States, controversy between religious groups has been comparatively mild. But the conflict between the Protestant majority and Catholic minority in Northern Ireland leads to daily violence and frequent

[20] Something of the range of variation in the historical legacy of differences will be found in Marie R. Haug, "Social and Cultural Pluralism as a Concept in Social System Analysis," *American Journal of Sociology*, 73 (November 1967): 294–304. The author classifies 114 countries according to an Index of Pluralism designed to reflect the amount of heterogeneity in language, race, religion, sectionalism, and ethnic groups.

killing. In the Middle East, an almost impenetrable tangle of conflicts involve Moslems, Jews, and Christians, Israelis and Arabs, Moslem Arabs in Iraq and Moslem (but nonArab) Iranians, Sunni Moslems and Shiite Moslems . . .

Finally, different stages of development tend to generate different forces stimulating cleavages and coalitions. In the nineteenth century, urbanization and industrialization in western European countries were accompanied by the misery and conflict that Marx was confident would finally polarize into a clear-cut conflict between an expanding urban proletariat and a decreasing capitalist bourgeoisie in which the proletariat was bound to win. Yet from the perspective of a later century, it appears that Marx was too hasty in extrapolating the early phases of industrialization into the indefinite future. Marx witnessed western Europe during the Industrial Revolution. He accurately foresaw that political conflicts would take place over demands for transforming the circumstances of the urban working classes. What he did not foresee was that long before the "bourgeoisie" was defeated in a conflict with the proletariat, three things would happen: The Industrial Revolution would begin to be transformed into a stage of high mass-consumption; the industrial proletariat would shrink in size and become an increasingly smaller minority of the total working force[21]; and because many demands put forward by leaders of the working classes would be met, the industrial proletariat, a minority, would become increasingly unresponsive to militant appeals for revolutionary change.

Yet in countries now passing through the Industrial Revolution, conflicts over demands for ameliorating or transforming the situation of urban workers are likely to be a prominent feature of political life. Meanwhile, new social and ideological bases of conflict are emerging in the high mass-consumption societies.

THE SEVERITY OF CONFLICT

The severity of conflict varies over time within any given system and from one system to another during the same period of time. Whatever difficulties may lurk in this proposition must not be allowed to obscure the fact that on common-sense grounds the proposition is hardly open to doubt. More than a century ago, Americans were engaged in killing one another on a massive scale in a civil war: That obviously was a severe conflict. The coup in Indonesia in 1966 in which the Sukarno regime was overturned and several hundred thousand people were killed was unquestionably a severe conflict. Armed rebellion, civil war, violent revolution, guerilla warfare, street bat-

[21] It does not follow, however, that the working classes have become a minority. For a presentation of statistics to the contrary, see Andrew Levison, *The Working Class Majority* (New York: Coward, McCann & Geoghegan, 1974).

tles, mass exile: These are conflicts of exteme severity. Speeches, debates, peaceful assembly, and peaceful elections are not.

Within any particular country, the temperature of political conflict fluctuates. Even the most stable countries are likely to have had a time of great turbulence and violence, a time of uprising, regicide, internal war—a "time of troubles." But the temperature of politics also fluctuates over short time periods. The Civil War marks the period of our most extreme conflict, but there has also been a conflict of considerable severity about once a generation throughout our national history, beginning with the Alien and Sedition laws at the end of the first decade under our Constitution.

During any particular period of time, however, some countries are more peaceful than others in their internal politics. While some countries may be passing through their historic Time of Troubles, others are basking in a mood of reconciliation and unity. It is even plausible that national differences in culture and temperament may make people in some countries more prone than those in others to seek peaceful, consensual solutions to their disputes. However that may be, it is clear that in any particular decade, conflict is more severe in some countries than in others.

Naturally, it is not easy to design satisfactory measurements for a concept such as "severity of conflict," nor to gather and interpret the data.[22] A half century ago, a pioneering effort of this kind was carried out by a sociologist, Pitirim A. Sorokin. Despite the high level of his work, his findings have been largely neglected. Sorokin applied intelligently designed indicators of "disturbances" in French history from A.D. 526 to 1925, as well as to Ancient Greece, Ancient Rome, Byzantium, Germany and Austria, England, Italy, Spain, the Netherlands, Russia, Poland, and Europe as a whole. From his enormous and painstaking studies, Sorokin concluded:

> On the average in most countries studied, for every year with a significant social disturbance there have been only five years free from disturbances.
>
> It is not true that some nations are more orderly than others: all nations are orderly and disorderly, according to the times.
>
> While there are some differences among nations with respect to the violence and intensity of disturbances, these differences are neither great nor consistent.
>
> Only about 5 percent of all the disturbances on record occurred without violence; about a fourth occurred with slight violence, however. The possibilities of a "bloodless revolution," it seems, are slight.
>
> Most disturbances last only a few weeks.
>
> The indicators show no continuous trend either toward bigger and better "orderly progress" or toward ever-increasing disorderliness.
>
> There is no association between internal disturbances and international war.
>
> Disturbances occur not only in periods of decay and decline of society but in periods of blossoming and healthy growth.

[22] For an account of recent research and theory, see Ted Robert Gurr, ed., *Handbook of Political Conflict: Theory and Practise* (New York: The Free Press, 1980).

> What is crucial is the sociocultural network of values and relations: When the network is integrated and strong, disturbances are at a minimum.[23]

More recently, other social scientists have returned to this important topic. In 1969, in a report to the United States National Commission on the Causes and Prevention of Violence, a political scientist compared the amount of conflict in 114 countries. He found that between 1961 and 1965 the magnitude of civil strife varied from ravaging civil wars and extensive mass violence in countries like the Congo, Indonesia, and South Vietnam to a total absence of any record of civil conflict in such countries as Sweden, Romania, Norway, and Taiwan.[24] Comparisons with the United States during its exceptionally turbulent years from 1963 to 1968 are shown in Table 6–3.

INSTITUTIONS FOR SHARING AND EXERCISING POWER

Finally, *political systems differ in their institutions for sharing and exercising power.* Many of us believe a corollary: that *political systems also differ in the distribution of power*—in the extent to which, in Aristotle's terms, power is distributed to one, few, or many. But given the problems in observing and measuring power discussed in Chapter 3, belief in this corollary must rest almost entirely on indirect evidence. And the most persuasive indirect evidence is the difference in the institutions that provide opportunities for citizens to share in the process of making policies enforced by the Government.

The processes by which governmental policies are made are exceedingly complex. Decisions of the Government seem to be reached as a result of some combination of direct or indirect participation by citizens, activists, and elites, acting through persuasion, threats, promises, direct manipulation, adaptation, deceit, and coercion. But the balance among these elements varies a great deal; the institutions unquestionably do.

They vary in two respects that are particularly crucial for sharing and exercising power. One of these is suffrage. This century has witnessed an all but worldwide acceptance of the belief that citizens of any country have the right to participate in governing that country by means of voting. Conse-

[23] Pitirim A. Sorokin, *Social and Cultural Dynamics*, vol. 3 (Boston: D. C. Heath & Co., 1937), Chap. Fourteen.

[24] Ted Robert Gurr, "A Comparative Study of Civil Strife," in Hugh Davis Graham and Ted Robert Gurr, *The History of Violence in America: A Report to the National Commission on the Causes and Prevention of Violence* (New York: Bantam Books, Inc., 1969), pp. 572–632. See also Ivo K. Feierabend, Rosalind L. Feierabend, and Betty A. Nesvold, "Social Change and Political Violence: Cross-National Patterns," pp. 632–87 of the same volume.

TABLE 6-3 Civil Strife in the United States During the Turbulent Sixties, Compared with Other Nations

	UNITED STATES	17 DEMOCRATIC EUROPEAN NATIONS	113 COUNTRIES
Pervasiveness: No. participants per 100,000 population	1,116	676	683
Rank of the U.S.		7th	27th
Intensity: Casualties from strife per 10 million population	477	121	20,100
Rank of the U.S.		3rd	53rd
Duration: Rank of the U.S.		1st	6th
Total Magnitude of Civil Strife: Rank of the U.S.		1st	24th
Rank of the U.S., 1961-1965		5th	41st

The figures for the United States are for 1963–68; for other countries, 1961–65.

Source: Ted Robert Gurr, "A Comparative Study of Civil Strife," in Hugh Davis Graham and Ted Robert Gurr, *The History of Violence in America; A Report to the National Commission on the Causes and Prevention of Violence* (New York: Bantam Books, 1969), pp. 572–632, Table 17-2, p. 578, and Table 17–15, p. 628.

quently only a half-dozen countries formally deny suffrage to their citizens today. Among the countries that grant suffrage, however, there are significant variations in the proportions of adults who are entitled to vote, and who do in fact vote. In the United States, for example, because of legal exclusions, barriers, or inconveniences caused by residence and registration requirements (and until recently because of the legal, semilegal, and illegal exclusion of Blacks), the proportion of the population of voting age who vote in national elections is lower than in almost every other representative democracy in the world.[25]

Another important axis is the extent to which those who are closest to the actual making of a governmental decision must compete for the votes of the electorate in unrigged elections, in which those who oppose the conduct of the Government can compete on equal terms. Thus it is possible to distinguish countries, or other political systems, by the extent to which law, constitution, custom, and political practice protect (1) freedom of expression, (2) freedom to form and join organizations, (3) access to alternative sources of information, (4) free and fair elections, (5) competition by political leaders for support and votes, and (6) institutions for making government policies dependent on votes and other expressions of preference.

Because countries have differed and continue to differ along both these axes—the extent of suffrage and freedom of opposition—the world provides a

[25] Taylor and Hudson, *World Handbook*, Table 2.8, p. 55.

vast array of political systems. At one extreme are countries that deny suffrage and suppress all opponents of the government. Let us call these *closed* (because most people are excluded from political life) *hegemonies* (because opponents are suppressed and the leaders of the government cannot be challenged by people outside the small closed circle of leadership). At the other extreme are countries that grant universal or nearly universal suffrage to all adults, and protect all of the six institutions listed in the last paragraph. In ordinary language we refer to such systems as "democracies," and call the countries "democratic countries." If we understand that in using these terms we are simply referring to countries with the six institutions listed above, no confusion need arise. But because the term "democracy" is also used to label an unattained, and perhaps unattainable, ideal, to apply the term to existing systems invariably leads to confusion and controversy. Consequently here and in later chapters, I depart from ordinary usage and use the terms "popular government" and "polyarchy" (literally, "rule by the many") to refer to political systems with widespread suffrage and relatively effective protection for the six institutions. Examples of polyarchies are the United States, Britain, Canada, France, West Germany, the Scandinavian countries, Italy, and Japan. Of the approximately 150 countries independent in 1980, about two dozen were polyarchies and another half dozen might be called near-polyarchies. The rest range from repressive hegemonies that suppress every public expression of opposition to more tolerant mixed regimes with varying degrees of freedom for the opponents of the government.[26]

What are the conditions in which polyarchies or popular governments are likely to be transformed into hegemonies? What are the conditions in which hegemonies are likely to be transformed into popular governments?

These questions direct attention to a problem that is not only one of the oldest in the study of politics, but also one of the most urgent and difficult in the contemporary world.

[26] Typically, for example, even mixed regimes that tolerate considerable freedom of expression for critics and opponents do not permit the existence of organized opposition parties.

7

POLITICAL REGIMES: POPULAR AND HEGEMONIC

In Chapter 5 we concluded that one similarity among political systems is that they all undergo change. Until the First World War a common view, particularly among Americans, was that history was on the side of democracy: Gradually or by revolution, hegemonic regimes would be transformed into popular governments. The outcome of the first great revolution of the twentieth century, however, was not a polyarchy, but a hegemonic regime in Russia. In rapid succession the fledgling polyarchies gave way to Fascism in Italy, Nazism in Germany, and a military regime in Japan. After the Second World War, in most of the "Third World," hegemony, not polyarchy, became established.

What lies ahead for popular government? Is hegemony the wave of the future? Although our knowledge is too limited to justify an unqualified prediction, we can specify with some confidence a number of conditions that increase the chances of polyarchy. One can then make an informed guess as to where polyarchy is likely to exist in the future.

As we examine these conditions, it is important to remember that most regimes are neither polyarchies nor full hegemonies. If the flood of typologies described in the last chapter does nothing more, it should warn us against trying to classify all the mixed regimes in one specific category. However, we can usefully envision polyarchies and hegemonies as standing at a distance from each other with a number of regimes scattered between them. Ignoring inclusiveness, what serves to distinguish mixed regimes is that they are less tolerant of political oppositions than polyarchies but more tolerant of oppositions than hegemonies. The problem, then, is to determine the conditions likely to stimulate changes that move a country's regime toward polyarchy or toward hegemony. These conditions may also reinforce the stability of an existing regime. Thus when conditions that favor polyarchy are present in countries with polyarchal regimes, polyarchy is more likely to endure.

SOME DIFFERENCES THAT MAKE A DIFFERENCE

Let me call attention to several differences that are related to earlier chapters. Although an adequate evaluation of regimes must consider more than these differences, no satisfactory appraisal could ignore them. For they are among the differences that make a difference.

Differences in Forms of Influence

Autonomy vs. Control. Individuals and subsystems are more autonomous in relation to the Government of the State in polyarchies than in hegemonies. To be sure, this difference is partly true by definition. In effect, what we mean by a polyarchy is a system with a relatively higher tolerance for individual and organizational autonomy; by a hegemonic regime we mean a system with relatively lower subsystem autonomy. The rights to participate in and to oppose the government, the hallmark of polyarchy, require the State to tolerate and even protect autonomy both for individuals and for organizations.

As a consequence of these rights, organizations of untold variety tend to exist in polyarchies: private clubs, cultural organizations, pressure groups, political parties, trade unions, and so on. Many of these organizations actively seek to influence the government; many more can be mobilized when their members believe that crucial interests are threatened. By contrast, the development of autonomy threatens the nature of a hegemonic regime and the power of its leaders. Autonomous organizations are particularly dangerous. Hence in hegemonic regimes, organizations must be kept under the control of the government. Ultimately, in a hegemonic regime every individual and every organization is part of an all-embracing system of hierarchical controls. Although this limit is never reached in practice, it has sometimes been closely approached—for example, in the Soviet Union during the later period of Stalin's rule and in Germany under Hitler.

Persuasion vs. Coercion. In polyarchies, as opposed to hegemonies, political leaders rely more on persuasion and less on coercion.[1] Some forms of coercion are by definition excluded or minimized in polyarchies. A regime that imprisons the leaders of opposition parties or suppresses critical newspapers, for example, is by definition not a polyarchy. Conversely, by definition a polyarchy must provide its people with rights to participate in choosing and opposing political leaders. An inclusive polyarchy extends these rights to almost all the adult population.

That these differences distinguish polyarchies from hegemonic regimes merely by definition does not make them less significant, since they reflect actual differences among real systems. Moreover, the difference in the balance of persuasion versus coercion is a practical consequence of the differences in the political institutions themselves. A group that has an effective right to participate in the choice of political leaders is less likely to be coerced in a conflict than a group without this right. This is most obvious if the group is numerous enough to constitute a majority. As long as the institutions of popular government are unimpaired, any attempt to coerce a majority of the population would be certain to fail, since a coerced majority could simply vote against the incumbents at the next election and replace them with more responsive officials. Because of this situation, politicians in polyarchies are rarely so foolhardy as to support laws directed against a majority of the people; if they ignore popular opinion, it is likely to cost them dearly. Of course, since laws rarely enjoy unanimous support, in any regime some persons could be coerced by laws that deprived them of some previous opportunity, privilege, or right. But even if people who participate in decisions sometimes suffer from the outcome, those who cannot participate at all are even more likely to suffer. It seems improbable that the Constitutional Convention would have permitted slavery in America if the black people in this country had possessed the same rights to political participation that white Americans had. In order to impose white supremacy on the recently liberated slaves after the Civil War, southern Blacks were deprived of their newly acquired right to participate in politics.

In a polyarchy, it is usually difficult to coerce a large number of people, even if not a majority. For while extensive coercion places a strain on any political system, popular governments find it the most difficult. If civil disobedience on a grand scale, or even civil war, is to be avoided, a government engaged in coercing large minorities needs to have an imposing array of coercive forces at its disposal—a centralized and disciplined police system, a secret police, a compliant judiciary, military and bureaucratic establish-

[1] Although he uses a different typology of political systems, David Apter presents a similar argument in *Choice and the Politics of Allocation* (New Haven: Yale University Press, 1971), pp. 32–33, and passim.

ments ready to obey the government when "duty" requires the coercion of large numbers of fellow citizens, and a body of law, constitutional doctrine, and practices that permit the government to employ these forces.

So imposing an array of coercion in the hands of the government would be a permanent temptation to unscrupulous leaders and a standing danger to all opposition. Although it is conceivable that a popular government might coerce a large fraction of the population on infrequent occasions and survive, the more frequently it did so, the more reduced the chances of its survival would be. For example, when extensive coercion over Blacks was reestablished in the American South in the last quarter of the nineteenth century, in effect the South developed a dual political system in which whites operated a quasipolyarchy and black southerners lived under a repressive hegemony.

Reciprocal vs. Unilateral Control. Because effective rights to opposition and participation are diffused more widely in polyarchies than in hegemonies, individuals and groups enjoy more autonomy vis-à-vis the government, the opportunities for political leaders to employ coercion against their critics and opponents are more limited, persuasion is more readily available than coercion as a means of influence, and political leaders are more likely to be involved in networks of reciprocal influence. In polyarchies, government policies are likely to be settled by negotiation and bargaining. In hegemonic regimes, by contrast, the influence of leaders is more unilateral, and policies are more likely to be attained by hierarchy and command.

Differences in Levels of Conflict

Political Conflict vs. Civil Strife. It would seem reasonable to suppose that polyarchies would be subject to more conflict than hegemonies. In an important sense this is true: In polyarchies there is a great deal of overt political conflict. For example, opposing parties, factions, or candidates square off in an open attempt to defeat each other in a legislative body, in an election, or in the larger forum of public opinion. One might think that this high propensity for overt political conflict would push polyarchies into civil strife—that is, highly intensified, aggressive, polarized conflicts expressed in such forms as riots, sabotage, assassinations, coups d'etat, and civil or guerilla warfare.

Yet this is not the case. Although conflict is frequent in polyarchies, it occurs typically at a comparatively low level of intensity. As Table 7–1 shows, countries with lower levels of intensity in conflicts from 1948–1965 were predominantly polyarchies, while countries with higher levels were predominantly nonpolyarchies. As the authors of the study from which the data for Table 7–1 are taken concluded:

> It appears that permissive countries are predominantly stable and nonviolent . . . ; however, the moment a modicum of coercion sets in, the situation is reversed. Moderate use of force seems to act as a stimulant to internal tur-

TABLE 7-1 Polyarchy and Level of Conflict (84 countries, 1948-1965)

	LEVEL OF CONFLICT[a]					
	LOW 1	2	3	4	5	HIGH 6
Percent of total countries:						
Polyarchies[b] (N = 30)	100	77	60	23	9	0
Nonpolyarchies (N = 54)	0	13	40	67	91	100
Total: (%)	100	100	100	100	100	100
Total: (N)	2	13	15	31	22	1
As percent:						
of all polyarchies[b]	7	33	30	23	7	0
of all nonpolyarchies	0	6	12	44	37	1

Source: Ivo K. Feierabend with Rosalind L. Feierabend and Betty A. Nesvold, "The Comparative Study of Revolution and Violence," *Comparative Politics,* 5 (April 1973) p. 393.

[a] The authors refer to their scale as a measure of political instability. However, it is equally appropriate to describe it as a measure of the level of conflict, since "each successive scale point denotes a greater amount of political aggression and violence." For example, "dismissals or resignations of officeholders are assigned to scale position 1; peaceful demonstrations and strikes are ascribed scale position 2; riots and assassinations are at position 3; and large-scale arrests and imprisonments, at position 4. Revolts are included in scale position 5, while guerilla and civil war and revolution are located at scale position 6." (p. 396)

[b] The classification of countries as polyarchies or nonpolyarchies is my own. No country was classified as a polyarchy unless it remained so throughout the whole period. However, see footnote 2.

moil . . . Furthermore, it would seem that the pacifying effect of coercion takes hold only among extremely coercive regimes. . . . It seems that, at least in the global sense, coerciveness at first stimulates violence until a certain point is reached. Then coerciveness, in the form of tyranny, seems probably just as apt to bring internal peace as more violence. . . .

The obvious conclusion from this cross-national study of violence and coerciveness would indicate that political regimes that resort to force, especially if they use force inconsistently, must expect political instability and violence. On the other hand, the odds are overwhelmingly in favor of political stability for consistently permissive regimes.[2]

In countries with popular governments, then, overt political conflict tends to be frequent but comparatively peaceful. In nonpolyarchies, overt

[2] *Ibid.*, p. 415. It is worth noting that the twenty-four countries classified by the authors as "permissive" were all polyarchies; of the twenty-three classified as coercive, none was a polyarchy; of the twenty-six classified as moderately coercive, only three (Chile, India, and Lebanon) were polyarchies. In all three, polyarchy was precarious. Chile subsequently fell to a severely repressive military dictatorship. In 1975, Lebanon was torn by acute internal violence that destroyed its delicate polyarchy. In mid-1975, the Indian prime minister, Indira Gandhi, proclaimed a state of national emergency under which she jailed hundreds of political opponents, including most of the leaders of the opposition parties, and imposed the harshest press censorship in India's history, even as a British colony.

political conflict may be less frequent but it is also likely to be more intense and violent. In polyarchies, political conflict is typically terminated by negotiation; in nonpolyarchies, by coercion. The characteristic mode of dealing with political conflict in polyarchies is by means of peaceful adjustment, while in nonpolyarchies it is by means of violence.

Differences in Institutions for Sharing and Exercising Power

How are we to account for the fact that in polyarchies, political conflicts tend to be handled by peaceful adjustment? As we know, some institutions are deliberately created to foster peaceful adjustment. The United Nations, for example, was intended to provide a forum for the peaceful adjustment of international conflicts. The countries of the European Common Market have developed institutions for settling many of their differences over economic questions. But for long centuries before these developed, an institution for encouraging consultation, negotiation, and the exploration of mutually beneficial solutions had already existed. This was the national parliament or legislature. The growth of a legislature, constitutionalism, and political parties has provided modern polyarchies with a complex network of procedures, traditions, rituals, and pressures involving elected representatives, leaders of interest groups, and experts, who mediate the conflicts among the manifold interest groups of modern society. It seems reasonable, then, that:

> The likelihood of peaceful adjustment to a conflict is increased in polyarchies by institutional arrangements that encourage consultation, negotiation, the exploration of alternatives, and the search for mutually beneficial solutions. Conversely, the prospects of violence are increased in nonpolyarchies by institutional arrangements that severely inhibit such activities.

But may it not also be the case that the prospects for polyarchy are also better in countries where people settle their conflicts peacefully? Or are both polyarchy and peaceful adjustment products of the same causes—historical experiences, for example, or high levels of economic development? Although once again one must accept the unhappy fact that reliable knowledge about this crucial matter is fearfully limited, there is convincing evidence that the kinds of differences mentioned in the last chapter do influence the chances of both polyarchy and peaceful settlement. We have just referred to one of these, political institutions.[3] Let us turn now to some of the others.

[3] Limitations of space compel me to ignore a rapidly growing body of theory and data bearing on a key political institution, the system of political parties, and how it relates to cleavages, conflicts, and polyarchy. The reader may wish to consult Joseph LaPalombara and Myron Weiner, *Political Parties and Political Development* (Princeton, N.J.: Princeton University Press, 1966); Seymour Martin Lipset and Stein Rokkan, ets., *Party Systems and Voter Alignments: Cross-National Perspectives* (New York: The Free Press, 1967); Erik Allardt and Stein Rokkan, eds., *Mass Politics* (New York: The Free Press, 1970).

Paths to the Present. Because the path that each country has taken to the present is unique, every country has a different legacy of conditions bearing on the chances for polyarchy and peaceful adjustment. In a sense, much of the rest of this chapter is an attempt to find patterns of explanation in these richly different historical legacies.

Three variations are particularly noteworthy. Two of these—the legacy of subcultures and the treatment of the working classes—are elements in a larger set of explanatory factors that will be dealt with separately. A third is the historical process of change. In some countries, violent revolutions (particularly revolutionary wars for national independence) have helped to unite a people, while in other countries revolutions have left enduring cleavages. Compare the results of the American Revolution and the creation of the Irish Free State, later the Republic of Ireland. In each case a violent struggle against Britain led to independence. In America, however, the Revolution, the armed struggle against the British, the mass exodus of British colonials, and the development of a widely shared republican ideology helped to foster unifying myths and left few divisive scars among the American people. But in Ireland the peace treaty in 1921 that preserved Protestant North Ireland as an integral part of the United Kingdom led immediately to fierce conflicts between the government of the new Irish Free State and the Irish Republican Army (I.R.A.) and then to persistent and bloody conflict in North Ireland between Protestant Irish and Catholic Irish, with the I.R.A. acting in violent support of the Catholic minority.

In a different perspective, some countries have enjoyed centuries of national independence in the course of which they have been able to accumulate political experience, develop their institutions, generate loyalties, break down cultural cleavages, establish a sense of nationhood, and work out ways of accommodation in their conflicts. Other countries have only recently become independent after decades or centuries of foreign rule and colonialism. These countries are new, still struggling to achieve a national identity, and still passing through the Time of Troubles. Racked by open or potential conflict, still unable, so their elites believe, to afford the luxury of polyarchy, leaders rely heavily on coercion to keep the nation and its institutions intact.

"Modernity": The Socioeconomic Level. One of the most powerful influences on a political system is the "modernity" or socioeconomic "level" of a country. Thus, Table 7–2 shows that relatively modern countries have a markedly lower level of conflict than countries with traditional societies or countries in transition from traditionalism to modernity.[4] Not surprisingly, the transitional countries have the highest level of conflict. Therefore:

[4] See also Ivo K. Feierabend, Rosalind L. Feierabend, and Betty A. Nesvold, "Social Change and Political Violence: Cross-National Patterns," in Hugh Davis Graham and Ted Robert Gurr, *The History of Violence in America* (New York: Bantam Books, 1969), pp. 632–87.

TABLE 7-2 Economic Development and Level of Political Conflict—118 countries, 1948-1977

	POLITICAL CONFLICT			
GNP PER CAPITA	LOW	HIGH	TOTAL: PERCENT	NUMBER
Low	58%	42%	100%	38
Middle	42%	58%	100%	62
High	61%	39%	100%	18
Total Number	(59)	(59)		(118)

Source: Charles Lewis Taylor and David A. Jodice, *World Handbook of Political and Social Indicators, Third Edition, Vol. 1: Cross National Attributes and Rates of Change* and *Vol. 2: Political Protest and Government Change* (New Haven: Yale University Press, 1983). Reprinted by permission of Yale University Press.

> Among the countries of the world, the chances for peaceful adjustment of political conflicts are higher, the greater the per capita Gross National Product and other indices of "modernization" associated with per capita GNP.

It is even less open to doubt that, statistically speaking, there is strong association between the socioeconomic level of different countries and the frequency of competitive politics in general and polyarchy in particular:

> Among the countries of the world, the frequency of competitive political systems and polyarchies is higher, the greater the per capita Gross National Product and other variables associated with per capita GNP.[5]

For example, in Chapter 6 we saw how 141 countries could be roughly divided into five levels of socioeconomic development (Table 6–2). In GNP per capita, around 1980 they ranged from Bhutan ($80), to Switzerland ($12,990). It turns out that at Level I (lowest GNP per capita) there are only two polyarchies, while at Level V (highest GNP per capita) every country is a polyarchy (Table 7–3).

Another example: If we compare the 38 polyarchies with the 103 non-polyarchies, we find that polyarchy is associated not only with higher GNP per capita but with greater urbanization, a smaller agricultural population, a higher literacy rate, and greater newspaper circulation (Table 7–4).

These and other data support the following observations:

(1) Below a minimum threshold of GNP per capita, the chances of competitive politics, and hence polyarchy, appear to be so low that variations in per capita GNP no longer matter.

(2) Above a maximum threshold, the chances of competitive politics and

[5] A list of sources bearing on this point will be found on p. 147.

TABLE 7-3 The Association between Polyarchy and Level of Socioeconomic Development—141 countries, 1980

LEVEL (GNP PER CAPITA, 1978)	ALL COUNTRIES			POLYARCHIES		
	NUMBER	RANGE	MEDIAN	NUMBER	PERCENT OF ALL COUNTRIES AT SAME LEVEL	PERCENT OF ALL POLYARCHIES
I	18	$ 80- 190	$ 155	2	11%	5%
II	26	$ 200- 380	$ 260	1	4%	3%
III	45	$ 410- 1310	$ 680	4	9%	10%
IV	37	$1440- 5720	$ 2850	16	43%	42%
V	15	$7160-12,999	$10,035	15	100%	40%
TOTAL	141			38		100%

Source: Charles Lewis Taylor and David A. Jodice, *World Handbook of Political and Social Indicators, Third Edition, Vol. 1: Cross National Attributes and Rates of Change.* (New Haven: Yale University Press, 1983). Reprinted by permission of Yale University Press.

polyarchy are so high that variations in per capita GNP do not seem to matter very much.

(3) However, the chances for competitive politics and polyarchy by no means depend entirely on socioeconomic levels, for there are too many exceptions and anomalies to be accounted for.[6]

TABLE 7-4 The Association between Polyarchy and Six Specific Indicators of Socioeconomic Development—141 countries, 1980

	PERCENTAGE OF:	
INDICATOR	POLYARCHIES	NONPOLYARCHIES
Per capita GNP $2850 or over	66%	9%
High degree of urbanization	63%	26%
Agricultural population under 33%	68%	41%
Agricultural population over 66%	3%	36%
Literacy rate of 50% or more	95%	46%
Newspaper circulation of 100 or more per thousand population	50%	11%

Source: Charles Lewis Taylor and David A. Jodice, *World Handbook of Political and Social Indicators, Third Edition, Vol. 1: Cross National Attributes and Rates of Change.* (New Haven: Yale University Press, 1983). Reprinted by permission of Yale University Press.

[6] Some of the deviant cases—particularly India, Sri Lanka, The Philippines, and Turkey—may now be seen as somewhat less deviant than they appeared to be in the 1960s. See footnote 2, above.

The most dramatic deviant case is that of the United States. In the early nineteenth century, when polyarchy took root in the U.S., this country was extremely "underdeveloped" according to most of the indices currently used to compare socioeconomic levels. It has been estimated that in 1800, American GNP per capita was $231 (in 1965 prices)—that is, less than that of Guatemala or El Salvador ($640) in 1980. The population of the United States was overwhelmingly engaged in agriculture. Urbanization was extremely low—only about 6 percent of Americans lived in places with 2500 or more people; and of course most of the other indices used to define the socioeconomic level of a country were equally "unfavorable." Yet in spite of these unfavorable indices, a polyarchy was successfully launched.

On the other hand, by 1980, the USSR and most of the other countries of Eastern Europe within the Soviet orbit had become highly industrialized countries with relatively high levels of GNP per capita. Yet they all retained one-party hegemonic regimes. Thus by 1980, per capita GNP in the Soviet Union had reached $3710 and in East Germany $5670, both well beyond that of the United States in the nineteenth century.[7]

(4) Furthermore, evidence does not support the view that above the upper threshold of development, there is an ever-increasing "democratization," as this might be measured by a variety of possible indices of "democracy."[8] For example, until recently the United States has enjoyed the highest GNP per capita in the world, but in comparison with other polyarchies, it has also had one of the lowest rates of voter turn-out in national elections and one of the worst records for excluding and coercing a large minority.

Equality and Inequality: The Distribution of Political Resources. Political theorists have generally insisted that a high degree of social and economic equality is a prerequisite for a democracy. "Allow neither rich men nor beggars," Rousseau wrote in *The Social Contract*. "These two estates, which are naturally inseparable, are equally fatal to the common good; from the one come the friends of tyranny, and from the other tyrants. It is always between them that the public liberty is put up to auction; the one buys, and the other sells."

Existing popular governments fall considerably short of the democratic ideal, but even they would be threatened seriously by extreme inequalities in the distribution of political resources, for these would produce great differ-

[7] Data on the U.S. population are from Bureau of the Census, *Historical Statistics of the United States* (Washington: Government Printing Office, 1969), p. 14. GNP data for the USA and USSR are from Charles Lewis Taylor and David A. Jodice, *World Handbook of Political and Social Indicators, Third Edition, Vol. 1: Cross National Attributes and Rates of Change* (New Haven: Yale University Press, 1983).

[8] On this point, see Deane E. Neubauer, "Some Conditions of Democracy," *American Political Science Review*, 61 (December 1967): 1002–9, and comments by Neubauer and Phillips Cutright in the same journal, 62 (June 1968): 578–81.

ences in the potential coercive power of different citizens. If this general line of reasoning is correct, what are the consequences of different levels of socioeconomic development on the distribution of political resources, and hence on the chances of polyarchy?

> The way in which political resources are distributed among the people of a country tends to vary with its level of socioeconomic development. With some important exceptions, inequalities in the distribution of political resources are greatest in countries with agrarian societies, less in industrial countries, and least in countries at the stage of high mass-consumption.

Let us examine this proposition in more detail by considering some of the characteristics of countries at different "stages" of socioeconomic development.

Countries at a very early stage of development usually lack even the rudimentary institutions required to sustain competitive politics. For example, such countries typically have a very high rate of illiteracy and lack the economic and social resources (such as a supply of full-time teachers) needed to provide a formal elementary education for the young.

Countries below the lower threshold are overwhelmingly agrarian, and even above this threshold the economy and society reflect the predominance of the agricultural section.

Agricultural societies are particularly prone to cumulative inequalities, for the value of the land a person owns not only determines total wealth and income but pretty much fixes social status, educational opportunities, and political, administrative, and military skills. Hence in an agricultural society, if the distribution of landed property is highly unequal, the distribution of all political resources and skills tends to be highly unequal; consequently, the distribution of power also tends to be highly unequal.[9] This is why a popular government is unlikely to exist in an agricultural society unless landed property is widely distributed with a considerable measure of equality. This point was first stressed explicitly by James Harrington, a seventeenth-century English writer whose ideas were accepted by many of the men at the American Constitutional Convention. Harrington wrote in *Oceana* (1656):

> Such as is the proportion or balance of dominion or property in land, such is the nature of the empire.
>
> If one man can be sole landlord of a territory, or overbalance the people, for example, three parts in four, he is Grand Seignoir; . . . and his empire is absolute monarchy.

[9] The causal arrow may run the other way. This is the argument of Gerhard Lenski in his spacious and well-buttressed analysis of the distribution of "power and privilege" in societies of various types: "Without exception, one finds pronounced differences in power, privilege, and honor associated with mature agrarian economies. . . . The very unequal distribution of power, privilege, and honor in them arises largely from the function of their political systems. To put it more plainly, in these societies, the institutions of government are the primary source of social inequality." *Power and Privilege* (New York: McGraw-Hill Book Company, 1966), p. 210.

> If the few or a nobility, or nobility with clergy, be landlords, or overbalance the people to the like proportion . . . the empire is mixed monarchy.
> And if the whole people be landlords, or hold the lands so divided among them that no one man, or number of men, within the compass of the few or aristocracy, overbalance them, the empire . . . is a commonwealth.

In short, according to Harrington, the distribution of power parallels the distribution of property (in land). One can witness this phenomenon today in many areas of the world that are predominantly agricultural, such as Central America. In a study of the relation of landholdings to politics in forty-seven countries, Russett found a marked correlation between inequality in land distribution and dictatorship or other forms of nonpolyarchy.[10]

Because polyarchies are heavily concentrated in countries beyond the agrarian stages, while nonpolyarchies are concentrated in countries predominantly agrarian, it is sometimes supposed that urban, industrial societies are more favorable to polyarchy than agricultural societies. Yet as the history of the United States and several other countries makes clear, an agrarian society is not per se inimical to polyarchy. Quite the contrary: An agrarian society that is pervaded by a considerable measure of equality can sustain the institutions of polyarchy, as the example of the United States demonstrates. But the circumstances that make for equality in an agrarian society are evidently rare.

Could the United States have developed and maintained institutions of popular government during the period when it was predominantly agricultural if it had not had its vast open frontier, which enabled nearly everyone who wished to do so to acquire land? Probably not. "The chief circumstance which has favored the United States," Alexis de Tocqueville wrote in 1835, "is the nature of the territory that the Americans inhabit. Their ancestors gave them the love of equality and of freedom; but God himself gave them the means of remaining equal and free, by placing them upon a boundless continent."[11]

As a country moves from earlier toward later stages of development, agriculture is displaced increasingly by commerce and industry. Although in the typical developing country political resources become somewhat less cumulative and no longer so fully monopolized by a small elite, conflicts increase as hitherto dormant sectors of the population develop rising expectations and begin to demand more education, economic security, steady employment, social and economic equality, recognition, participation, democracy, and so forth. In short, as conditions favorable to competitive politics and polyarchy develop, so do the number and intensity of conflicts. Thus a competitive political system may begin to develop only to be swamped by conflicts it cannot handle.

[10] Bruce M. Russett, "Inequality and Instability: The Relation of Land Tenure to Politics," *World Politics* 16 (April 1964): 442–54.

[11] Alexis de Tocqueville, *Democracy in America* 1 (New York: Vintage Books, 1955), p. 301.

Later, however, as a country becomes more fully industrialized, it develops an economic "surplus" well above subsistence needs, which can be drawn on to facilitate peaceful adjustment of conflicts. Even if the number of conflicts remains high, their intensity declines as many of the older grievances are met, the most humiliating and aggravating inequalities are reduced, people come to expect that new conflicts probably will be settled by reasonably satisfactory compromises made possible by the "surplus," and political resources become so widely dispersed (though still unequally distributed) that few wholly defenseless groups remain.

To be sure, "subsistence" and "surplus" are not precise terms. What a villager in India might regard as quite adequate for subsistence, an American would regard as totally inadequate. Nonetheless, common sense tells us that the average American middle-class family has a much greater "surplus" to dispose of than the family of a villager in India; likewise, the United States in toto has a greater "surplus" to dispose of than India does—which is one reason why we once provided foreign aid to India rather than the other way around.

How does the existence of a "surplus" facilitate adjustment? Essentially by increasing the number of conflict situations to which there are mutually profitable solutions. A surplus makes it easier for parties in a conflict to be "bought off."[12] For example, employers find it easier to grant wage increases and other benefits to workers; as a consequence the intensity of labor disputes is lessened. Conflicts over allocating government revenues to social services, military expenditures, and subsidies to business and agriculture can be resolved by giving everyone a slice out of rising revenues from an expanding economy. Conversely, violence and civil strife are likely to increase whenever a surplus declines or disappears. A surplus diminishes if the quantity of goods and services available declines (as in an economic depression), if the requirements for "subsistence" increase (as a result of changes in attitudes and ideas current in a society), or if both happen.[13] This helps to explain why many revolutions and other civil disturbances have followed times of *rising* prosperity, for during long periods when standards of living are rising, new expectations are created; the grinding poverty of the past is no longer acceptable. Hence when economic decline or stagnation encounters a rising curve of expectations, revolution or other forms of civil strife are likely to increase.[14]

[12] For American experience on this point, see David Potter, *People of Plenty* (Chicago: University of Chicago Press, 1954), p. 122.

[13] In *Why Men Rebel* (Princeton, N.J.: Princeton University Press, 1970), Ted Robert Gurr puts the "intensity of relative deprivation" at the center of his explanation of "the potential for collective violence." Gurr distinguishes three different patterns of relative deprivation: "*decremental deprivation*, in which a group's value expectations remain relatively constant but value capabilities are perceived to decline; *aspirational deprivation*, in which capabilities remain relatively static while expectations increase or intensify; and *progressive deprivation*, in which there is substantial and simultaneous increase in expectations and decrease in capabilities." (p. 46).

[14] James C. Davies, "The J-Curve of Rising and Declining Satisfactions as a Cause of Some Great Revolutions and a Contained Rebellion," in Hugh Davis Graham and Ted Robert Gurr, *The History of Violence in America: A Report to the National Commission on the Causes and Prevention of Violence* (New York: Bantam Books, 1969), pp. 690–730.

Thus there appear to be two different ways of reducing cumulative inequalities and increasing the chances of popular government. One way, suggested by Harrington in England, Rousseau in France, and Jefferson in the United States, is by decreasing the degree of inequality in the distribution of political resources—for example, through land redistribution, tax reforms, and expansion of educational opportunities. Although many countries have moved in this direction, so far none has managed to eliminate sizable differences with respect to at least some key political resources, whether these are income, education, mass media, party membership, or others. The other way is by dispersing the inequalities that remain, so individuals or groups badly off with respect to some kinds of resources are better off with respect to others. This seems to be the pattern that exists in the United States and probably in a number of other mature industrialized nations. The two solutions are not, of course, mutually exclusive: A high stage of industrialization may tend to strengthen both patterns, not only by decreasing the extreme inequalities that are mainly a legacy of early industrial systems superimposed on feudalism, but also by dispersing the remaining advantages or handicaps to different groups.

However, even in high mass-consumption societies where inequalities are dispersed sufficiently to enable polyarchy to exist, the inequalities that persist are likely to be a source of discontent and of demands for greater democratization. As a result, new patterns of conflict may arise in countries at the high mass-consumption level. Though it waned as quickly as it waxed, the widespread involvement of university students in demonstrations, sit-ins, and strikes in the late 1960s may well have marked the onset of this new stage. Just as advanced industrialization favors political democratization in the shape of polyarchy, the stage of high mass-consumption and beyond may encourage further efforts to democratize many institutions—political, social, economic, educational—in which inequalities persist.

Bases of Cleavage: Subcultures. As we have seen, countries differ in the extent to which the past has left a legacy of subcultural differences in religion, ethnic groupings, race, and language, and of memories of past treatment of these differences. Both aspects are important.

> The level of consensus in a country, and hence the chances of peaceful adjustment and polyarchy, are influenced both by the degree of subcultural diversity and by the way that differences in subcultures are dealt with.

A legacy of subcultural differences increases the area of potential conflict. The fact that New Zealand, Sweden, Norway, and Iceland are culturally quite homogeneous helps to account for their relatively low levels of conflict. Conversely, India's innumerable subcultures contribute heavily to its high level of conflict. It is not surprising, then, that polyarchies are much more common in homogeneous countries than in countries with numerous subculture cleavages (Table 7–5).

TABLE 7-5 Polyarchy and Subcultural Cleavages

	AMOUNT OF SUBCULTURAL CLEAVAGE			
	LOW	MODERATE	MARKED	EXTREME
Total countries	26	28	27	33
No. of polyarchies	15	10	3	6
Polyarchies as percent of total	58%	36%	11%	18%

Note: The table is based on my classification of polyarchies and data on subcultural cleavages from Marie R. Haug, "Social and Cultural Pluralism as a Concept in Social System Analysis," *American Journal of Sociology*, 73 (November 1967): 294–304. In the table above, low is defined as 0 or 1 on Haug's index, moderate as 2 or 3, marked as 4 or 5, and extreme as 5, 6, or 7.

But the ways in which countries deal with their subcultural differences also help to explain levels of agreement and conflict. If the level of conflicts is higher in Belgium than in Switzerland, for example, much of the explanation can be found in the fact that Switzerland, with four language groups, two religions, and strong cantonal loyalties has managed to avoid serious discrimination among its subcultures. By contrast, Belgium still suffers from several centuries of discrimination of Walloons against Flemings. The United States, while relatively successful in avoiding conflicts among a people marked by religious and ethnic diversity, has a record unequaled in any other polyarchy of discriminating against inhabitants of African origin, both as slaves and citizens. This legacy of discrimination was a direct cause of the civil strife over the rights and opportunities of Afro-Americans that swept the United States in the 1960s.

THE NEXT STAGE?

In different countries, the various factors we have been examining interact in different ways. The interactions sometimes engender offsetting effects. More frequently, perhaps, they reinforce one another, and thereby dramatically raise or lower the chances for polyarchy and peaceful adjustment.

Looking over the analysis of this chapter, the reader may be tempted to believe that an inexorable historical evolution terminates in peaceful polyarchies. Reverting again to Russett's typology, everything seems to work against polyarchy and peaceful settlement of conflicts during the first three stages. For example, extreme cultural diversity, with all that differences in subcultures imply for coercion and conflict, is the typical lot of less developed countries. Thus among forty-nine countries at a relatively low level of urbanization (that is, where less than 20 percent of the population live in cities over 20,000), over half fall into the last category in Table 7–5, indicating an extreme degree of subcultural cleavage. By contrast, among more urbanized countries, only about 12 percent have an extreme degree of social and cultural diversity. Literacy rates show a similar relationship.

To look at the relationship the other way round, countries with an extreme degree of subcultural diversity are also relatively "underdeveloped." For example, three-fourths of the thirty-three countries classified as having an "extreme" degree of subcultural cleavage also have a per capita GNP under $150; among twenty-six countries with a negligible degree of subcultural cleavage, only one has such a low GNP. Or again: 70 percent of the countries with extreme subcultural diversity gained independence after 1945, whereas 72 percent of the countries with negligible diversity gained independence before 1914.[15]

Countries at the Industrial Revolution stage are, as we have seen, subject to conflict over demands for improving the lot of the expanding proletariat. Moreover, the way the grievances of manual workers, both urban and rural, are dealt with in the process of industrialization leaves a legacy of resentment or loyalties. In Italy and France, for example, the failure of governments to respond vigorously to working-class demands left a powerful residue of resentment toward the social, economic, and political orders. In New Zealand, Britain, Australia, Sweden, Norway, and Denmark, vigorous and generous responses cemented the allegiance of manual workers to the prevailing institutions.

As countries approach the stage of mass-consumption, antagonisms seem to decline and areas of agreement increase. Some critics argue that what results is not so much a rational or spontaneous consensus as a manipulated or pseudoconsensus.[16] However that may be, there is impressive evidence that the process does take place.[17] Yet it would be hazardous to project this trend indefinitely into the future. Certain kinds of questions, such as foreign policy and the distribution of power, income, wealth, and other forms of privilege, do not lend themselves to technical solutions or to final answers. Around such questions, it is reasonable to think, new conflicts and new ideologies will emerge—may, indeed, have begun to emerge already—even in countries of greatest affluence.[18]

There is good reason to think that even when countries reach the stage of high mass-consumption, or whatever may prove to be the next stage as the twenty-first century approaches, politics by no means will disappear. There will be new cleavages, new ideologies (or old ones dressed in new clothes), and new conflicts. There can be no guarantee that these conflicts will be set-

[15] Marie R. Haug, "Social and Cultural Pluralism as a Concept in Social System Analysis," *American Journal of Sociology*, 73 (November 1967): 294–304.

[16] Herbert Marcuse, *One Dimensional Man* (Boston: Beacon Press, 1964).

[17] Robert E. Lane, "The Politics of Consensus in an Age of Affluence," *American Political Science Review*, 59 (December 1965): 874–95.

[18] See Robert A. Dahl, ed., *Political Oppositions in Western Democracies* (New Haven: Yale University Press, 1966), pp. 398–401.

tled peacefully, that democratic ideals will be realized more fully, that new polyarchies will emerge, or even that existing polyarchies will survive. Yet it is not unreasonable to hope that as our knowledge about the central questions of this chapter increases, people will be able to act more wisely to reduce coercion, adjust their conflicts peacefully, and improve the performance of governments, as measured against the exacting and unachieved standards of democracy.

8

POLITICAL MAN

A starting point for all political theory is the fact that members of the human species live together. With few exceptions, human beings do not live in complete isolation. Whatever may be the elements of instinct, habit, necessity, or choice that induce people to form societies, they have demonstrated amply for thousands of years that the human being is a social animal. Yet, although they are social animals, neither by instinct nor by learning are they necessarily political animals—at least not in quite the same sense. Even though they live in a society, they need not concern themselves with the politics of that society, nor participate actively in political life, nor cherish the political institutions and values of the society. Some people do but many do not.

Nonetheless, because human beings are social, they develop political systems. Evidently they cannot dwell together without entering into relationships of influence. Whenever these relationships become stable and repetitive, political systems exist.

In this looser sense, then, one might say (with Aristotle) that man *is* a political animal. Whatever their values and concerns, people are inevitably enmeshed in political systems—whether or not they like or even notice the fact.

However, the individuals who find themselves within the boundaries of a political system are by no means equally concerned with political life. Some people are indifferent to politics; others are deeply involved. Even among those who are heavily involved in politics, only some actively seek power. And among the power-seekers, some gain more power than others. These four groups—the apolitical stratum, the political stratum, the power-seekers, and the powerful—are shown in Figure 8–1.

THE APOLITICAL STRATUM

Since the apolitical stratum shades off imperceptibly into the political stratum, an exact boundary between the two must be arbitrary. Nonetheless, they are, as we shall see, distinguishable.

Because many of us take it for granted that people are naturally political animals, the existence of active and involved citizens, who make up the political stratum, hardly seems to need an explanation. What is more puzzling is the presence of an apolitical stratum.

It appears to be true, nonetheless, that in most political systems those who show great interest in political matters, are concerned and informed about politics, and are active in public affairs, do not make up a large proportion of adults; usually, it appears, they are a minority. Even in countries with popular governments where opportunities for political involvement are extensive, the political stratum by no means includes all the citizens. On the

FIGURE 8-1
Political Strata

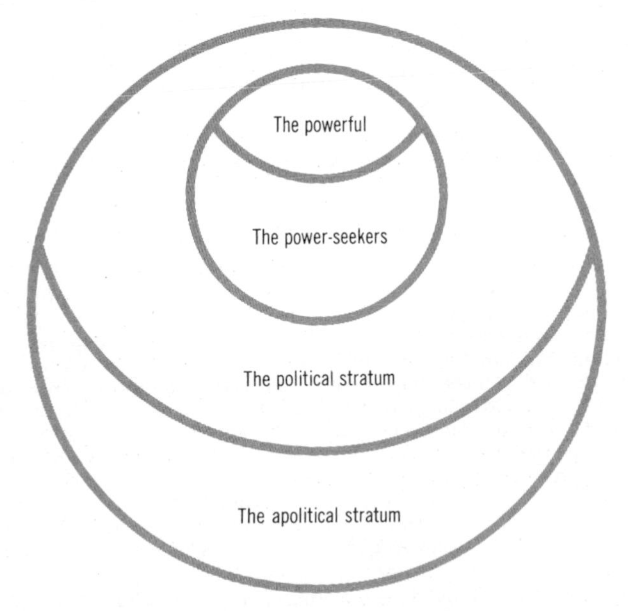

contrary, in all polyarchies, it seems, a sizable number of citizens are apathetic about politics and relatively inactive. In short, they are apolitical.

To be sure, there are significant variations from one system to another and from time to time. Yet the failure of a considerable body of citizens to take advantage of opportunities to participate in political life seems to be a nearly universal phenomenon. Even the Greek city-sates, which are sometimes held up as models of democratic participation, were not immune. In Athens, for example (where the majority of adults—women, foreigners, and slaves,—were excluded from participation), the male citizens who made up the *demos* evently included a sizable apolitical stratum. If one compares the conjecture of a number of scholars that the demos in the fifth century B.C. consisted of around thirty to forty thousand persons with the estimate that there were only eighteen thousand seats on the Pnyx, where the Assembly of all citizens met, and the fact that a quorum for some purposes was six thousand, then it seems obvious that a large proportion of the demos ordinarily did not attend the Assembly meetings. In fact, "to ensure adequate attendance at a dull Assembly meeting, police with long ropes dipped in wet paint herded citizens to Pnyx Hill," where the Assembly met.[1] By Aristotle's time a century later, citizens received six obols a day for attending the Assembly, the town meeting of Athens.[2] Sometimes New England town meetings are regarded as models of democratic participation. But just as in Athens, in New England towns many citizens were unconcerned about exercising their rights or fulfilling their political obligations.[3] Even today the problem is acute. In most polyarchies, between a fifth and a third of the eligible voters usually do not vote in national elections, and much larger fractions abstain from other kinds of political activity. Only about half the adults in the United States and Germany, and still fewer in Britain, France, Italy, and Mexico, follow public affairs in newspapers or on the radio or television.[4]

[1] C. M. Bowra, *Classical Greece* (New York: Time, 1965), p. 108. The figures in the preceding sentence are from Bowra, on the page cited, and H. D. F. Kitto, *The Greeks* (Baltimore: Penguin Books, 1951, 1957), p. 131.

[2] Aristotle, *On the Constitution of Athens*, Appendix IV in Ernest Barker, ed., *The Politics of Aristotle* (New York: Oxford University Press, 1962), pp. 379–83.

[3] In New Haven, for example, the problem seems to have been a persistent one. In 1642 the General Court of the Colony "voted that any freeman who after due warning, should fail to appear in the General Courts before the Secretary finished the roll-call, should be fined ls, 6d; and that any of the rest of the planters who should be absent after their names were read, should be fined one shilling. The novelty of the first few years had worn away, and attendance at the General Courts seemed, to many, burdensome." A century later the problem was still unsolved in New Haven. In 1784 the old colonial town officially became a city, and the first city elections were held. Of some 600 men living in the city, about 250 were excluded as voters either because they could not meet the property requirements or because they had been loyal to Great Britain. Of the 343 eligible men, about one-fourth failed to take the oath and hence could not vote in the first election. Although most of those who were qualified to vote did actually vote for the mayoralty candidates, two days later only about a hundred citizens (out of 261 eligible) showed up to vote for the councilmen. Charles H. Levermore, *The Republic of New Haven* (Baltimore: John Hopkins University Press, 1886), pp. 44, 231.

[4] Gabriel A. Almond and Sidney Verba, *The Civic Culture* (Boston: Little, Brown & Company, 1965), Table II.5, p. 56; and Philip E. Converse and Georges Dupeux, "Politicization

Why is it that even in modern societies with widespread education, universal suffrage, and democratic political systems the apolitical stratum is so large? To answer this question would require much more space than can be given here, but a short if somewhat formal answer can be given.[5] There seem to be several fundamental reasons why people do not become involved in politics.

(1) *You are less likely to get involved in politics if you place a low value on the rewards expected from political involvement relative to the rewards you expect from other kinds of activity.* The rewards a person may gain (or expect) from political activity can be conveniently divided into two kinds: *direct gratifications* received from the activity itself and *instrumental benefits* brought about as a consequence of the activity.

Direct gratifications from political involvement include the sense of fulfilling one's obligations as a citizen, the pleasures of social interaction with friends and acquaintances, heightened self-esteem from contact with important persons or access to inside information, the excitement of politics as a game or contest in which one's side may win or lose, and so on. For many people, however, political activity is a good deal less gratifying than other outlets —for example, family, recreation, friendships formed at work or in one's neighborhood. For many, political involvement yields far less affection, income, security, respect, excitement, and other values than working at one's job, watching television, reading, fishing, playing with the children, attending a football game, or assembling a new hi-fi set. The explanation, no doubt, lies in the fact that people are not by instinct reasonable, reasoning, civic-minded beings. Many of our most imperious desires and the source of many of our most powerful gratifications can be traced to ancient and persistent biological and physiological drives, needs, and wants. Organized political life arrived late in human evolution; today people learn how to behave as political participants with the aid, and often with the hindrance of instinctive equipment that is the product of a long development. To avoid pain, discomfort, and hunger, to satisfy drives for sexual gratification, love, security, and respect are insistent and primordial needs. The means of satisfying them quickly and concretely generally lie outside political life.

Instrumental benefits expected from political activity may be divided roughly into two kinds. Some are special benefits for a particular person or family—a job from party leaders, pay for being a pollwatcher, graft, and so on. Or the benefits may be favorable government decisions: "the government issues a zoning variance to an individual so that he can enlarge his home, pro-

---

of the Electorate in France and the United States," in Angus Campbell, Philip E. Converse, Warren E. Miller, and Donald E. Stokes, *Elections and the Political Order* (New York: John Wiley & Sons, Inc., 1966), pp. 269–91.

[5] A much more complete analysis can be found in the comprehensive study of participation in the United States by Sidney Verba and Norman H. Nie, *Participation in America: Political Democracy and Social Equality* (New York: Harper & Row, 1972).

vides a license, grants an exemption from the army because of a family hardship, removes an unsightly telephone pole, offers agricultural assistance or agrees to provide a better water supply to a given home."[6] For some people, special benefits provide a sufficient incentive for political participation. The old-fashioned American political machine built the loyalty of its followers and party workers essentially on special benefits.

But particularized benefits rarely are extended widely enough to involve the whole citizen body. All that most citizens hope to gain from government are collective benefits (costs)—consequences of decisions that affect a large category of persons such as tax payers, social security beneficiaries, automobile drivers, and so on. In decisions about war and peace, foreign affairs, military policy and a number of other matters, the collectivity may include virtually the whole citizen body. However, some people do not believe that they stand to benefit from these governmental activities. In a survey of political attitudes and activities of citizens in four polyarchies and one regime dominated by a single party (Mexico), about three-quarters of the people in the United States and Britain thought the activities of the national government tended to improve conditions in the area, about half thought the same in Germany and Italy, and a sixth in Mexico. The rest were in varying degrees hostile, doubtful, uncertain, or without an opinion.[7] For some persons, then, the rewards of political involvement are distant and vague, whereas the rewards of other activities are more immediate and concrete.

In short, for many people the opportunity costs of political involvement are simply too high to make it worthwhile. These people are unwilling to forego immediate, certain, and concrete benefits or gratifications derived from nonpolitical activities to obtain the more remote, uncertain, and abstract benefits that might ensue from political participation.

(2) *You are less likely to get involved in politics if you think that there is no significant difference in the alternatives before you and, consequently, that what you do won't matter.* Thus people who say they don't care "which party wins the presidential election this fall" are much less likely to vote in American presidential elections than those who say they care a good deal.[8] Some people fail to vote or otherwise participate in politics because they believe the parties do not offer them a real choice. This view may be more common among Americans than among citizens of some other polyarchies. For example, in a comparison of Americans and Norwegians, among Americans "40 percent thought the two parties were about the same, and an additional 8 percent didn't know whether they differed or not." By contrast,

[6] *Ibid.*, p.49. The distinction between the two forms of participation described in this and the following paragraph is taken from Verba's and Nie's discussion.

[7] Gabriel A. Almond and Sidney Verba, *The Civic Culture* (Boston: Little, Brown & Company, 1965), Table II.3, p. 48

[8] Angus Campbell, Philip E. Converse, Warren E. Miller, and Donald E. Stokes, *The American Voter* (New York: John Wiley & Sons, Inc., 1960), p. 104.

among the Norwegians, only "11 percent felt that there were no differences between the parties; an additional 8 percent did not know whether there were differences or not.[9]

(3) *You are less likely to become involved in politics if you think that what you do won't matter because you can't significantly change the outcome anyway.* A great many surveys have demonstrated a strong relationship between the confidence that what one does really matters and the extent of one's political involvement. The weaker one's "sense of political efficacy," the less likely one is to become involved.[10]

The confidence one has in one's capacity to be effective in political life depends on many factors. Confidence may, of course, reflect a realistic appraisal of a situation. It is hardly surprising that people who see an upcoming election as a completely one-sided affair are less likely to vote than those who believe that it is going to be close. Even people who care a great deal about the outcome of an election may decide not to vote if they believe that the election is too one-sided for their vote to make any difference.[11] Nor should it be too surprising that in a number of countries people are likely to have more confidence in their capacity to be effective in changing the conduct of government at the local level than at the national level.[12]

Whether the judgment is realistic or not, many citizens are weighed down by a sense that officials just won't pay attention "to people like me." In the United States, political self-confidence—the sense of political efficacy—tends to increase, the higher one's income, social standing, political experience, and, most of all, education.

Probably one's "personality" has some bearing on one's sense of efficacy. Optimism or pessimism about one's chances of influencing policy probably is related to deeper personality factors, such as an underlying sense of confidence that pervades a person's entire outlook.[13] One's political confidence, or lack of it, may feed on itself. A person lacking in confidence may avoid politics, thus decreasing one's chances of being effective and further diminishing one's confidence. Conversely, a confident person may, as a result of political involvement, grow even more confident.

(4) *You are less likely to become involved in politics if you believe that the outcome will be relatively satisfactory to you without your involvement.*

[9] Angus Campbell and Henry Valen, "Party Identification in Norway and the United States," in Campbell et al., *Elections and the Political Order* (New York: John Wiley & Sons, Inc., 1966), p. 258.

[10] Campbell et all, *The American Voter*, p. 105, and Robert R. Alford and Harry M. Scoble, "Sources of Local Political Involvement," *American Political Science Review* 62 (December 1968), pp. 1192–1206, at p. 1200.

[11] Campbell et. al., *The American Voter*, Table 5.3, p. 99.

[12] Robert A. Dahl and Edward R. Tufte, *Size and Democracy* (Stanford, Calif.: Stanford University Press, 1973), pp. 53–65.

[13] Campbell, et al., *The American Voter*, pp. 516–19.

A citizen who believes a particular political decision is important, nevertheless might not become involved in it if he or she feels quite confident that the decision will turn out well anyway. Just as low confidence in one's political efficacy discourages participation, so too, high confidence in the all-round justice legitimacy, stability, and fairness of decisions in one's political system may make one's participation seem unnecessary.

(5) *You are less likely to get involved in politics if you feel that your knowledge is too limited for you to be effective.* In every country, it seems, large numbers of people feel they do not understand politics very well.[14] It is not surprising that some of them turn away from politics entirely.

(6) *Finally, the greater the obstacles placed in your way, the less likely you are to become involved in politics.* When people expect high rewards from an activity, they are willing to overcome great obstacles and incur high "costs" to gain them. But when they believe the rewards are going to be low or nonexistent, even modest obstacles and costs are enough to discourage them. Why bother to climb over a fence if the grass is not greener on the other side?

Thus there is good reason for thinking that the markedly low turnout in national elections in the United States, as compared with almost all other countries, is caused partly by an additional barrier to voting—registration requirements. In other countries citizens do not have to "register" or may do so in a simple, convenient, almost automatic way. In the United States, differences in registration procedures and requirements tend to effect the percentage of the population of voting age that registers.[15] Seemingly small matters make a difference. For example, according to one estimate, extending the closing date from one month before the election day to one week "would tend to increase the percentage of the population registered by about 3.6 percent."[16]

The costs of political involvement also may vary with different activities. As Verba and Nie have emphasized, some activities, such as campaigning, involve conflict with other participants; people who dislike conflict, then, are more likely to stay away from these forms of participation. In addition, they point out, some activities—getting in touch with an official, for example—require much more initiative than does voting.[17] It is hardly surprising that voting is far more common than citizen-initiated contacts with officials.

[14] Dahl and Tufte, *Size and Democracy*, Table 4.8, p. 54.

[15] Steven J. Rosenstone and Raymond E. Wolfinger, *Who Votes?* (New Haven: Yale University Press, 1981).

[16] Stanley Kelley, Jr., Richard E. Ayers, and William G. Bowen, "Registration and Voting: Putting First Things First," *American Political Science Review* 61 (June 1967): 367.

[17] Verba and Nie, *Participation in America*, pp. 50–51.

THE POLITICAL STRATUM

All the forces we have just examined also can work in reverse. It seems obvious that you are *more* likely to become involved in politics if you:

1. value the rewards to be gained
2. think the alternatives are important
3. are confident that you can help to change the outcome
4. believe the outcome will be unsatisfactory if you don't act
5. have knowledge or skill that bears on the question at hand
6. must overcome fewer obstacles to act.

Because of these and other factors, some people *are* interested in politics, *are* concerned and informed about politics, and *do* participate in political life. These people constitute the political stratum.

Yet the same forces seem to operate within the political stratum: Some people are much more interested, concerned, informed, and active than others. In countries with popular governments in which citizens are legally free to participate in a wide variety of political acts, the more demanding, the more time-consuming, costly, or difficult the activites are, the smaller are the numbers who engage in them. Citizens are much more likely to vote, for example, than to attend a political meeting, more likely to attend a meeting than to work actively for a candidate or party. Few citizens try to influence an act of the national legislature or, for that matter, the more accessible officials of the local government (see Table 8–1).[18] In the most complete study of political participation among Americans, (see Table 8–2), Verba and Nie have shown that "voting in Presidential elections is the only participatory act out of our rather extensive list of activities that is performed by a majority of those interviewed."[19]

In addition, however, Verba and Nie discovered a phenomenon that had been largely overlooked in previous studies of participation: There is a significant degree of specialization within the political stratum. They found that Americans could be divided into six types:

The Inactives (22 percent) who take "almost no part in political life." These are equivalent to our apolitical stratum.

[18] For example, for France, see Converse and Dupeux in *Readings in Modern Political Analysis*, p. 408. For Britian, see Richard Rose, *Politics in England* (Boston: Little, Brown & Co., 1964), p. 89. For a comparison of Norway and the United States, see S. Rokkan and A. Campbell, "Citizen Participation in Political Life: A Comparison of Data for Norway and the United States of American," in *Decisions and Decision-Makers in the Modern State*, J. Meynaud, ed. (Paris: UNESCO, 1967), pp. 254–5.

[19] Verba and Nie, *Participation in America*, p. 31.

TABLE 8-1 Percentage Who Say They Have Attempted to Influence the Government (by Country)

COUNTRY	LOCAL GOVERNMENT[a]	NATIONAL LEGISLATURE[b]	N
U.S.	28%	16%	970
U.K.	15	6	963
Germany	14	3	955
Italy	8	2	995
Mexico	6	3	1295

Source: Almond and Verba survey, unpublished data.

[a] "Have you ever done anything to try to influence a local decision?"
[b] "Have you ever done anything to try to influence an act of the [national legislature]?"

The Voting Specialists (21 percent) who vote in Presidential elections but do little else. While this single activity distinguishes them from the inactives, the fact that they *only* vote also distinguishes them sharply from participants who do something *in addition* to voting.

The Parochial Participants (4 percent) who not only vote but also make particularized contacts with government officials for *special* benefits. However, they engage in no other forms of participation.

TABLE 8-2 Percentage of Amercians Engaging in Twelve Different Acts of Political Participation

TYPE OF POLITICAL PARTICIPATION	PERCENTAGE
1. Report regularly voting in Presidential elections	72
2. Report always voting in local elections	47
3. Active in a least one organization involved in community problems	32
4. Have worked with others in trying to solve some community problems	30
5. Have attempted to persuade others to vote as they were	28
6. Have ever actively worked for a party or candidates during an election	26
7. Have ever contacted a local government official about some issue or problem	20
8. Have attended at least one political meeting or rally in last three years	19
9. Have ever contacted a state or national government official about some issue or problem	18
10. Have ever formed a group or organization to attempt to solve some local community problem	14
11. Have ever given money to a party or candidate during an election campaign	13
12. Presently a member of a political club or organization	8

Source: Sidney Verba and Norman H. Nie, *Participation in America: Political Democracy and Social Equality,* Table 2–1, p. 31. Copyright © 1972 by Sidney Verba and Norman H. Nie. Reprinted by permission of Harper & Row, Publishers, Inc.

The Communalists (20 percent) who not only vote but also engage in community action for *collective* benefits. The Communalists, however, do not engage in campaign activites.

The Campaigners (15 percent), "the mirror-image of the communalists. These citizens engage in almost no communal activity but are most active in political campaigns."

The Complete Activists (11 percent) who "engage in all types of activity with great frequency."[20]

Thus the members of the political stratum are far from a homogeneous lot. They differ enormously not only in the volume but also in the form of their participation in political life. While it is true that the complete activists are a comparatively small minority, the Verba and Nie findings do show that half of all American citizens engage in some kind of political activity in addition to voting. Altogether, the political stratum in the United States appears to consist of about three-quarters of the adult population.

THE POWER-SEEKERS

Within the political stratum, some persons seek power much more vigorously than others. And some persons gain much more power than others. In short, within the political stratum, there is a substratum of power-seekers and a substratum of powerful leaders.

You will notice that what we have just said is a restatement of two propositions set forth in Chapter 5 as empirical characteristics of political systems:

1. Some members of the political system seek to gain influence over the policies, rules, and decisions enforced by the government.
2. Political influence is distributed unevenly among the members of a political system.

Now, to seek power and to gain power are by no means the same thing. Not only are some power-seekers unsuccessful in their efforts but some people who gain power may not actually seek it—they might acquire it, for example, by inheritance.

We have, then, two important questions: Why do some people seek power more actively than others? And why do some gain more power than others?

Socioeconomic Status

Socioeconomic status is associated with all three factors that help to account for differences in influence: inequalities in resources, differences in skills, and

[20] Sidney Verba and Norman H. Nie, *Participation in America: Political Democracy and Social Equality*, pp. 79–80. Copyright © 1972 by Sidney Verba and Norman H. Nie. Reprinted by permission of Harper & Row, Publishers, Inc.

differences in incentives to use resources for gaining influence.[21] Therefore, it is not surprising that political activity tends to be greater among persons of higher socioeconomic status. In fact, Verba and Nie found that in the United States socioeconomic status accounts more than any other single factor for variations in levels of participation (Figure 8–2).

There is reason to think that socioeconomic status may be more highly related to participation in the United States than in many other polyarchies. Yet important as it is, even in the United States socioeconomic status accounts for only a rather small part of the variation in political activity.[22] Among persons of similar socioeconomic status and similar amounts of political resources some engage far more actively than others in the search for influence over government. Why?

The answers to this question can be grouped into three categories:

(1) *People seek power*, it is said, *in order to achieve the collective good.* They wish to protect the interest of all citizens, achieve justice for all,

FIGURE 8–2 Status Composition at Varying Levels of Participation

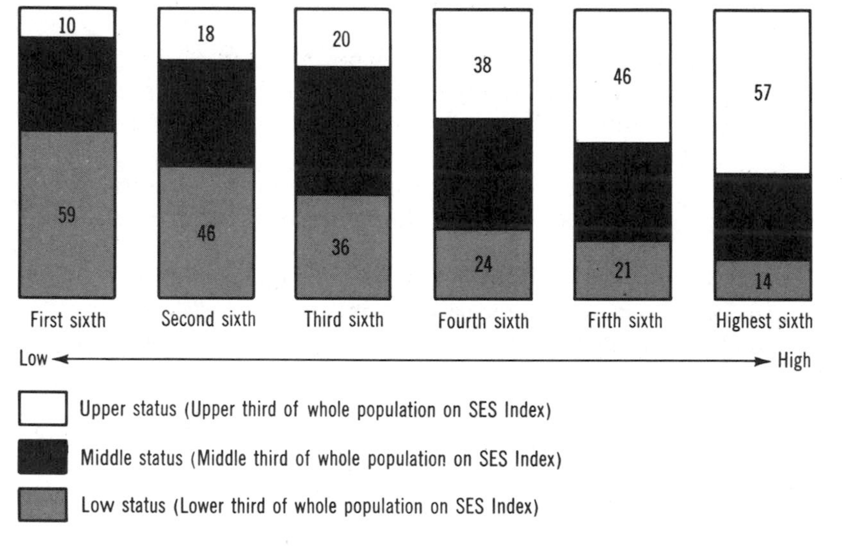

Source: Verba and Nie, *Participation in America,* Figure 8–3, p. 131. Reprinted by permission.

[21] Cf. Chapter 3, p. 32.

[22] For some international comparison, see Verba and Nie, *Participation in America,* Table 20–1, p. 340. They show correlations between participation and Socioeconomic status of .43 and .37 from two different studies. Socioeconomic status thus accounts for less than one-fifth the total variation—leaving 80 percent or more unaccounted for. Moreover, Rosenstone and Wolfinger (*supra*, footnote 15) show that in voting, education is far and away the most important component of socioeconomic status, so much so, in fact, that among voters with about the same level of education, variations in income and occupation account for very little. It is possible, however, that in forms of participation other than voting—such as getting in touch with officials—income and occupation might matter more than they do in voting.

benefit the state, or provide for life, liberty, and the pursuit of happiness. This is the argument attributed to Socrates in Plato's *Republic:*

> No science of any kind seeks or orders its own advantage, but that of the weaker which is subject to it and governed by it.
>
> [Thrasymachus] tried to fight this conclusion, but he agreed to this too in the end. And after he had, I said: Surely no physician either, in so far as he is a physician, seeks or orders what is advantageous to himself, but to his patient? . . .
>
> He said yes . . .
>
> Does it not follow that the ship's captain and ruler will not seek and order what is advantageous to himself, but to the sailor, his subject?
>
> He agreed, but barely.
>
> So then, Thrasymachus, I said, no other ruler in any kind of government, in so far as he is a ruler, seeks what is to his own advantage or orders it, but that which is to the advantage of his subject who is the concern of his craft; it is this he keeps in view; all his words and deeds are directed to this end.[23]

The difficulty with this debate between Socrates (or Plato) and Thrasymachus is that the two men are talking right past one another. This often happens in political controversy; each opponent vigorously flails an argument the other did not make, and thereby fails to meet head-on the precise point the other did make. In this case Socrates evidently intends his argument to be primarily *normative,* while Thrasymachus pretty clearly means his observation to be essentially *empirical.* Socrates met Thrasymachus' attempt to describe how rulers generally *do* act by indicating how good rulers *ought* to act.

Socrates and Plato knew perfectly well that rulers of states do not in fact always rule in the interests of their subjects. Indeed, to both Socrates and Plato the very meaning of a bad or perverted state was that the rulers did not seek the good of those over whom they ruled. Later on in the *Republic,* after describing how dictatorship evolves from democracy, Plato undertakes to explain how "the dictatorial man himself" develops:

> . . . Some of our unnecessary pleasures and desires seem to me lawless; they are probably present in everyone, but they are held in check by the laws and by the better desires with the help of reason. In a few men they have been eliminated or a small number are left in a weakened state, while in others they are stronger and more numerous.
>
> . . . What we want to establish is this: that there is a dangerous, wild, and lawless kind of desire in everyone, even the few of us who appear moderate. . . .
>
> This, my dear friend, I said, is precisely how a man becomes dictatorial, when his nature or his pursuits or both make him intoxicated, lustful, and mad.[24]

In sum, many political philosophers have argued that leaders *should* seek power in order to exercise authority for the good of all. But probably no

[23] *Plato's Republic,* trans. by G. M. A. Grube (Indianapolis: Hackett Publishing Co., 1974), lines 342d–343.

[24] *Ibid.,* lines 571b, 572b, and 573c.

student of politics has ever really argued that this is the only reason, or even the principal reason, why people *do* in fact seek power.

(2) *People seek power*, it has been argued, *in conscious pursuit of their self-interest.* This was the argument of Thrasymachus that Socrates purported to attack. Thrasymachus had said (according to Plato):

> I say that the just is nothing else than the advantage of the stronger . . . Do you not know . . . that some cities are ruled by a despot, others by the people, and others again by the aristocracy? . . . Yes, and each government makes laws to its own advantage: democracy makes democratic laws, a despotism makes despotic laws, and so with the others, and when they have made these laws they declare this to be just to their subjects, that is, their own advantage, and they punish him who transgresses the laws as lawless and unjust. This then, my good man, is what I say justice is, the same in all cities, the advantage of the established government, and correct reasoning will conclude that the just is the same everywhere, the advantage of the stronger.[25]

Thrasymachus may have represented an early Greek attempt to find naturalistic explanations for political behavior. Since nearly all we know of him comes from his enemy Plato, his argument in the *Republic* probably is somewhat distorted. Evidently Thrasymachus was trying to explain how it is that although rulers always proclaim that they are seeking justice, different rulers impose different ideas of justice on their states. To Thrasymachus the obvious explanation of the paradox was that each ruler was simply pursuing his own self-interest: "justice" as it was actually defined in the laws of each state was a mere ideological rationalization for the self-interest of the rulers. It is quite possible that Thrasymachus used his analysis to uphold traditional Athenian democratic institutions against subversion by supporters of oligarchy who insisted that they and they alone were concerned for the good of the state. Undoubtedly he also employed his analysis to undermine the appeal of Plato's elaborate defense of aristocracy, which Thrasymachus probably believed was no more than a brilliant rationalization for the antidemocratic ambitions of the oligarchical faction in Athens.[26]

Thrasymachus' hypothesis that people deliberately seek power for reasons of self-interest has been restated many times. Hobbes, for example, held that people were impelled by their passions and guided by their reason. Passion is the wind that fills the sails, reason the hand on the rudder. A human being, to use another metaphor, is a chariot pulled by the wild horses of passion and steered by reason. Human desires are insatiable, but reason dictates prudence. With the aid of reason, people can discover the general rules or precepts that will enable them to improve their chances of gaining the ends their passions dictate. All people, then, seek power in order to satisfy their

[25] *Ibid.*, lines 338c, d, e.

[26] On this point see Eric A. Havelock, *The Liberal Temper in Greek Politics* (New Haven: Yale University Press, 1957), p. 231 and *passim*.

passions. But reasons tells them *how* to seek power to reduce frustration, defeat, and the chances of violent death.

One difficulty with this hypothesis, as Plato rightly saw, is that the notion of "self-interest," which seems transparently obvious, is actually very complex. What one views as one's "self" depends on one's identifications, and evidently these vary a good deal. How one perceives the self is not wholly instinctive, it seems, but also a matter of social learning and personal development.[27] Likewise, what one considers to be in the "interest" of the self is shaped by learning, experience, tradition, and culture. Consequently, to attribute an act to self-interest does not explain very much. As a distinguished modern psychologist has said:

> The self comprises all the precious things and persons who are relevant to an individual's life, so that the term selfish loses its original connotation, and the proposition that man is selfish resolves itself into the circular statement that people are concerned with the things they are concerned with.[28]

Jones's self-interest can mean his pursuit of advantages for himself alone. Or it can mean his attempt to obtain advantages of all kinds for himself and his family. The Jones family now becomes the "self," and its "interests" run from acquisitiveness to zoology. Or Jones's self-interest can mean his attempt to obtain advantages for larger strata with which he identifies—his neighborhood, region, class, religion, ethnic group, race, nation. Thus both the "self" with which Jones identifies and the range of ends he regards as in the "interests" of the self may be extremely narrow or very wide, depending on learning, experience, tradition, and culture. Anthropological studies testify to the fact that notions of self, interest, and self-interest vary widely among human beings.

A second objection to rational self-interest as an explanation is posed by post-Freudian psychology. Thrasymachus, Hobbes, Bentham, and Marx all interpreted the search for power as "rational" and conscious pursuit of self-interest. But Freud showed that the "dangerous, wild, and lawless kind of" desires of which Socrates spoke do more than drive human beings into conflict with one another (as Hobbes argued); they also drive human beings into conflict with themselves. These inner conflicts, according to Freud, are fierce gales that often blow out the flickering light of reason. Reason, as Freud saw

[27] Psychologists such as Jean Piaget and his followers, who have carefully observed children, have concluded that the child's "ego" develops naturally through certain stages. See Piaget, *The Moral Judgment of the Child* (New York: The Free Press, 1948), and Erik Erikson, *Childhood and Society* (New York: Norton, 1950). The psychologist Lawrence Kohlberg contends further that human beings have a built-in predisposition to develop their moral understanding through certain stages. See his *The Philosophy of Moral Development*, Vol. I, (San Francisco: Harper & Row Publishers, Inc., 1981), and below, Chap. 9, fn. 31, p. 136.

[28] Gardner Murphy, "Social Motivation," in *Handbook of Social Psychology*, vol. 2, ed. G. Lindzey (Reading, Mass.: Addison-Wesley Publishing Co., Inc. 1954), p. 625.

it, cannot always guide the chariot drawn by passion, for these violent steeds turn on one another and in their battle the reins of reason become entangled.

Freud discovered, analyzed, and stated what those keen students of human psychology, the great playwrights and novelists, had always known. But since Freud's day, several social scientists have attempted to develop systematic theories dealing with the search for power.

(3) *People seek power*, some recent students of politics have argued, *from unconscious motives*. An explanations of power seeking along these lines is provided by Harold Lasswell. It can be summarized as follows: The power-seeker pursues power as a means of compensating for psychological deprivations suffered during childhood. Typical deprivations that engender power seeking are a lack of respect and affection at an early age. The self, then, suffers damage; the individual acquires a low estimate of himself or herself. (The self usually includes more than the "primary ego," the "I" or "me"; it includes parents, spouse, children, friends, fellow citizens, co-religionists, and others.) In childhood, adolescence, or perhaps later, power-seekers learn to compensate for this low estimate of the worth of "self" by pursuing power. They come to believe that by acquiring power they can either make the self better, and hence more loved and respected, or they can change the attitudes of others about that "self." With power they will become important, loved, respected, admired. They hope, then, to acquire through power relationships the affection and respect they failed to acquire in family relationships. None of this behavior, of course, need be impelled by conscious, "rational" thought. On the contrary, a great deal of the motivation is likely to be unconscious. Power-seekers do not necessarily have much insight into why they seek power; they rationalize this power-seeking in terms acceptable to their conscious values and perhaps the prevailing ideology among those with whom they identify. In comparison with other people, then, the power-seeker is a person who: (*a*) places a high value on gaining power; (*b*) demands power (and other values) for the self (the primary ego plus incorporated symbols of other egos); (*c*) has relatively high confidence about gaining power; and (*d*) acquires at least a minimum proficiency in the skills of power.[29]

Lasswell's characterization of the power-seeker is, however, subject to a number of qualifications, some of which Lasswell himself pointed out.

1. A power-seeker does not necessarily seek power in the Government; he may seek it in other institutions, such as business, the church, and the universities.
2. Extreme damage to one's self-esteem "may be beyond compensating," and may not produce a seeking for power but "resignation, withdrawal, and, in extreme cases, suicide."
3. A low sense of self-esteem may be sublimated in ways other than political activ-

[29] Harold D. Lasswell, *Power and Personality* (New York: W. W. Norton & Co., Inc., 1948), Chap. Three, "The Political Personality."

ity. One might, for example, be drawn to the stage and seek to become an actor worshiped by his public.

4. A person who seeks power to compensate for his own sense of inadequacy may not be effective in *achieving* power, since he is likely to stimulate too much dislike and distrust in others. "A person with a raging desire for power . . . will constantly alienate his supporters, thereby making the achievement of power impossible for him."
5. Survey research shows, as we have seen, that feelings of self-confidence and personal effectiveness are highly related to political participation; yet it seems unlikely that persons who feel self-confident and effective would also have a low sense of self-esteem.
6. Power can serve many ends. Hence one may seek power from many different motives; the need to compensate for a damaged sense of personal worth is only one of these.[30]

Of the three explanations for seeking power that we have explored, none seems entirely satisfactory. However, our discussion does suggest several conclusions:

First, whatever the reasons may be, some people do seek power more intently than others.

Second, scientific knowledge about the personalities and motives of power-seekers is still scanty. Everyone agrees that some people seek power more ardently than others, but authorities disagree over why they do.[31]

Third, depending on culture, society, economy, and political system, power (as Lasswell and many others have pointed out) can be used to acquire fame, reverence, security, respect, affection, wealth, and many other values. It is not surprising, then, that men and women should seek power; nor should we necessarily assume that power-seeking is abnormal or pathological. In its instrumental character, power is like money. Some people invest more effort in gaining money than others do; they do not necessarily do so because they value money, as such, more highly than others do, but because they see money as an instrument to other goals.

Fourth, power-seeking, like other behavior, no doubt is usually a com-

[30] These qualifications have been made by Harold D. Lasswell, "A Note on Types of Political Personality," *The Journal of Social Issues*, 24 (July 1968): 81–91, p. 84; Arnold A. Rogow and Harold D. Lasswell, *Power, Corruption and Rectitude* (Englewood Cliffs, N.J.: Prentice-Hall, Inc., 1963), p. 35; Robert Lane, *Political Life* (Glencoe, Ill.: The Free Press, 1959); pp. 126–127; Rufus Browning, "The Interaction of Personality and Political System in Decisions to Run for Office" *The Journal of Social Issues*, 24 (July 1968): 93–109; and Alexander L. George, "Powers as a Compensatory Value for Political Leaders," *The Journal of Social Issues*, 24 (July 1968): 29–49, at p. 49.

[31] The state of knowledge is best described in Fred I. Greenstein, *Personality and Politics* (New York: W. W. Norton & Co., 1975); in his chapter "Personality and Politics," in *The Handbook of Political Science*, vol 2, ed. Fred I. Greenstein and Nelson W. Polsby (Reading, Mass.: Addison-Wesley Publishing Co., Inc., 1975); and in the July 1968 issue of *The Journal of Social Issues*. The entire issue, under the editorship of Fred I. Greenstein, is devoted to Personality and Politics: Theoretical and Methodological Issues. See also Fred I. Greenstein and Michael Lerner, *Sourcebook for the Study of Personality and Politics* (Chicago: Markham, 1969).

pound of conscious and unconscious motives. People who seek power may know some of the reasons why they do so; we can hardly expect them to know all the reasons.

Fifth, it seems unlikely that all power-seekers have substantially similar personalities. There are too many different reasons, conscious and unconscious, why one might want power, and too many variations in the costs and benefits of power from one political system to another and from one time to another. Undoubtedly both Caligula and Abraham Lincoln sought power. Yet it is highly implausible to suppose that Caligula and Lincoln had even approximately the same kind of personality.

THE POWERFUL

Not all power-seekers, we have said, gain power. Indeed, although it is probably uncommon, some men and women who do not seek to gain and wield power may nevertheless exercise it. Why do some people gain more power than others?

In principle, if one gains more power than another (over X, with respect to Y) then we may look to two possible sources of explanation—to differences in the amount of resources used and to differences in the skill or efficiency with which the resources are applied. Some people use more resources to gain power than others do. Some people use what resources they have more efficiently, more skillfully.

Why do some people use more resources? Presumably because they expect to "gain more" by doing so. I may "gain more" than you from a given action either because the action is "less costly" to me or because the outcome of the action is "more valuable" to me. If A has more resources than B—for example, wealth—then a given outlay is less costly for A than for B (all other things being equal) because A has to forgo fewer alternatives than B. Or, in the language of the economist, A's opportunity costs are lower.

A person of wealth and a good deal of leisure can devote sixty hours a week to nonpaying political activities at considerably lower opportunity cost than a person who has to work long hours to make a living. In short, if A has more resources than B, the opportunity costs of allocating a given amount of those resources to gaining power are less for A than for B: A can make the same outlays as B at less opportunity cost or more outlays at the same opportunity cost. In general, then, some people *use* more resources to gain power than others do because they have *access* to more resources. And, all other things being equal, it is reasonable to expect that people with more resources will gain more power. To this extent, then, differences in power and power-seeking are related to differences in objective circumstances.

However, "all other things" are not usually equal. Even if their resources were objectively identical, A might allocate more resources in order to gain power if he or she placed a higher value on the results. Why might A place a higher value than B on the results of an outlay of resources to gain power?

1. Because A might expect different results from those that B expects
2. Because, though both expect the same results, A and B use different values or different scales to appraise the results
3. Because, though they expect the same results, A feels more confident about the outcome than B does

However, A's application of more resources may not result in more power (measured in any of the ways described in Chapter 3) if B has more skill than A. For a deft politician may accomplish more with little than a clumsy politician can accomplish with a great deal. Why then do some people have more skill in politics than others?

This is a difficult question to answer. To try to do so would carry us beyond the limits of this book. In brief, however, there are three possible causes for a difference in skill between two persons, whatever the skill may be, whether walking a tightrope over the Niagara, playing the part of Mimi in *La Bohême*, or serving as majority leader in the United States Senate. These are: (1) genetic differences; (2) differences in opportunities to learn; and (3) differences in incentives to learn. The first two are differences in situation, the third a difference in motivation.

We began this section with the question—"Why do some people gain more power than others?" Our answer is summarized in Figure 8–3.

VARIETIES OF POLITICAL MAN

Our examination of power-seekers and the powerful points up the seemingly endless variety of human motivations, incentives, orientations, and even personalities at work in political life. Attempts to impose a degree of intellectual tidiness on this disorderly array of human types have sometimes been notable for their insight and brilliance, but so far they have met with scant success. In recent years, however, social scientists have emphasized five factors that help to account for the variety of political types.

A particular person's orientations toward politics can be explained, to some degree, in the light of:

1. Personality or character
2. The general culture, or more specifically, the political culture, shared with others in the tribe, village, city, country, or world region
3. Early political orientations and how they are acquired—that is, *political socialization*

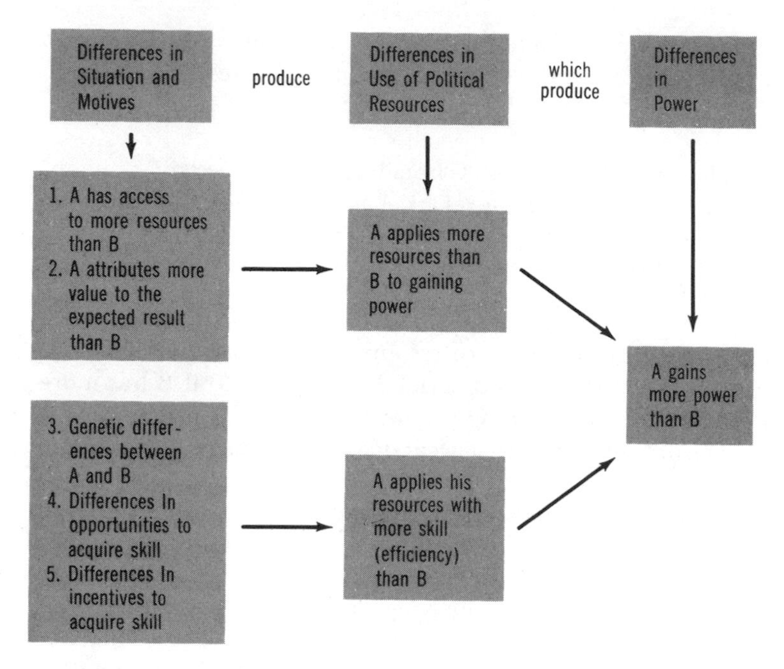

FIGURE 8-3 Why Some People Gain More Power than Others

4. Personal experiences and circumstances, life situations
5. The particular situation one confronts, or believes one confronts, at a specific historical moment

A consideration of several varieties of people in politics will help one to see how these five factors interact.

Democrat and Despot. Is it possible to specify a kind of personality or character that is especially suited—or unsuited—to the operation of popular government? Plato thought so; in *The Republic* he vividly sets out his description of the oligarchic, democratic, and dictatorial characters and offers explanations of how these come about.[32] In one form or another, Plato's general hypothesis has been affirmed many times—by Machiavelli, among others.[33]

Empirical information bearing on Plato's hypothesis is still lacking, despite a good deal of speculation that, at least in recent years, has been aided by the insights of modern psychiatry and psychoanalysis. Is there a "demo-

[32] This discussion takes place in Books 8 and 9. See Grube's translation, pp. 194 ff.

[33] For example, in his *Discourses on the First Ten Books of Titus Livius*, First Book, Chapters sixteen, seventeen, and eighteen, in Nicoló Machiavelli, *The Prince and the Discourses* (New York: Random House, Inc., 1940), pp. 160–68.

cratic" personality?[34] After examining a substantial body of work on the subject, one scholar remarks that "Almost all the modern students of national character are convinced the answer to this question is in the affirmative. Systematic evidence for this faith is unfortunately lacking."[35] Nonetheless, among recent students of politics who deal with this question, there is "an extraordinary degree of agreement about the values, attitudes, opinions, and traits of character" that help to maintain a popular system. The most important are attitudes toward one's self, toward others, toward authority, toward the community, and toward values:

1. *Toward self:* A belief in the worth and dignity of one's self
2. *Toward others:* A belief in the worth and dignity of others
3. *Toward authority:* A stress on personal autonomy and maintaining a certain distance from or even distrusting powerful authority; in contrast to the authoritarian, the absence of a need to dominate or submit
4. *Toward the Community:* Openness, ready acceptance of differences, willingness to compromise and change
5. *Toward values:* A pursuit of many values rather than a single all-consuming goal, and a disposition to share rather than to hoard or monopolize[36]

Is there an antidemocratic or despotic personality? Since 1950 a good deal of important exploratory work has been carried out on the characteristics of a syndrome termed the "authoritarian personality." A person is said to have an authoritarian personality if he or she is rigidly conventional; submissive and uncritical toward authority; agressive and punitive toward people who violate conventional values; opposed to subjective, imaginative, tender-minded ways of thinking about the world; preoccupied with power and toughness; cynical; concerned that wild and dangerous things are going on in the world; and particularly obsessed with sexual "goings-on."[37] Because of criticisms of the questionnaire used to tap these underlying attitudes—

[34] An excellent summary and critique of the leading theories is contained in Paul M. Sniderman, *Personality and Democratic Politics* (Berkeley: University of California Press, 1975), Chapter Five, "Democratic Commitment and the Democratic Personality," pp. 164–222.

[35] Alex Inkeles, "National Character and Modern Political Systems," in Francis W. K. Hsu, *Psychology and Anthropology: Approaches to Culture and Personality* (Homewood, Ill.: Dorsey Press, 1961), pp. 172–208.

[36] This list is adapted in slightly modified form from a list of Inkeles, *ibid.* Inkeles in turn draws heavily on Lasswell, whose work on democratic character is the modern seminal source. Cf. particularly Lasswell's *Democratic Character* in *The Political Writings of Harold D. Lasswell* (Glencoe, Ill.: The Free Press, 1951), pp. 465–525, and Fred I. Greenstein, "Harold D. Lasswell's Concept of Democratic Character," *Journal of Politics* 30 (August 1968): 696–709. See also Karl Mannheim, *Freedom, Power, and Democratic Planning* (New York: Oxford University Press, 1950), Chapter Nine, "The Pattern of Democratic Personality," pp. 228–45; and Robert Lane, "Notes on a Theory of Democratic Personality," in *Political Ideology* (New York: The Free Press. 1962), pp. 401–12.

[37] W. Adorno, Else Frenkel-Brunswik, Daniel J. Levinson, and R. Nevitt Sanford, *The Authoritarian Personality* (New York: Harper & Row Publishers, Inc., 1950), p. 228.

often called the F-scale—many scholars have been skeptical of studies describing the political behavior of people with authoritarian personalities. Some social scientists, however, have improved upon the earlier work by developing new concepts and measures.[38]

There is ample evidence to confirm the common-sense view that people do vary a good deal in authoritarianism, open-mindedness, dogmatism, rigidity, flexibility, and the like. Sometimes investigations have produced rather startling results: One study of Italian members of parliament, for example, found that communist deputies were very much less dogmatic than the deputies of any other party![39]

Yet the connection between personality and overt political actions remains complex, obscure, and apparently rather loose.[40] It is no doubt a reasonable hypothesis that a popular government would have great difficulty surviving in a population composed *mainly* of individuals with strongly "authoritarian personalities." But it is possible that political culture might significantly channel the outlets for a democratic or authoritarian personality. In a predominantly "democratic" culture, where democratic norms, institutions, and practices have a high degree of legitimacy, some individuals with "authoritarian personalities" may, conceivably, acquire an overlay of democratic beliefs and habits that help them function "democratically." Indeed, there is good reason for thinking that authoritarian or democratic orientations are very significantly shaped by culture and by processes of political socialization.[41] The authors of the five-nation study cited earlier in this chapter offer an impressive body of evidence for the conclusion that the political cultures of these five countries vary in significant ways, and that these differences have a bearing on the prospects of popular government.[42]

Conceivably, personality and character contribute less than political culture to the shaping of democratic—or despotic—persons. This view is supported by a recent study of the relationship between self-esteem and democratic orientations. Among three large samples of Americans—one of them consisting of political activists—Paul Sniderman found that "there are

[38] For an example, see Milton Rokeach, *The Open and Closed Mind* (New York: Basic Books, Inc., Publishers, 1960).

[39] Gordon J. DiRenzo, *Personality, Power, and Politics* (Notre Dame: University of Notre Dame Press, 1967), pp. 123–4. Robert D. Putnam found that in Italy deputies on the Left "are considerably more open in their partisanship than those at the Right. There is also a tendency, especially marked in Italy, for politicians of the Left to be more favorable to the principle of compromise. Indeed, among Italian Communists the acceptability of compromise solutions to political problems has become almost dogma. For some the dogma is probably only verbal, but for others it is deeply felt." *The Beliefs of Politicians: Ideology, Conflict, and Democracy in Britian and Italy* (New Haven: Yale University Press, 1973), p. 61.

[40] The best statement is Fred I. Greenstein, "The Impact of Personality on Politics," in *Personality and Politics*, footnote 20.

[41] An excellent comparison of Britain and Italy will be found in Robert D. Putnam, *The Beliefs of Politicians*.

[42] Almond and Verba, *The Civic Culture*.

indeed fundamental differences in psychological makeup between those who affirm the principles of democracy and those who fail to adhere as consistently to them. . . . The democrat is more likely to have high self-esteem and less likely to be hostile." However, Sniderman suggests that the linkage is less a matter of motivation than of social learning: Persons with high self-esteem are more likely to learn the norms of their culture, in this case the democratic norms that tend to prevail in the American political culture. It does not follow necessarily that in a different culture high self-esteem would lead to the adoption of democratic norms. On the contrary Sniderman argues:

> The same psychological qualities that distinguish a democrat in the United States may well characterize a communist in Soviet Russia; for insofar as the linkage between personality and political ideology is a matter of social learning, then high self-esteem (and conceivably many other personality traits as well) ought to drive individuals towards accepting the norms of their political culture, whatever those may be[43]

Agitator and Negotiator. Two other interesting varieties of political actors are the *agitator* and the *negotiator.* The classic description of the personality of the political agitator was presented by Lasswell in 1930:

> The essential mark of the agitator is the high value which he places on the emotional response of the public. Whether he attacks or defends social institutions is a secondary matter. . . . The agitator easily infers that he who disagrees with him is in communion with the devil, and that opponents show bad faith or timidity. Agitators are notoriously contentious and undisciplined; many reforming ships are manned by mutineers. The agitator is willing to subordinate personal considerations to the superior claims of principle. Children may suffer while father and mother battle for "the cause." . . . The agitator sees "unworthy" motives where others see the just claims of friendship. . . . [He] trusts in mass appeals and general principles . . . live[s] to shout and write. . . . [Agitators] conjure away obstacles with the ritualistic repetition of principles. They become frustrated and confused in the tangled mass of technical detail upon which successful administration depends. . . . They glorify men of outspoken zeal, men who harry the dragons and stir the public conscience by exhortation, reiteration, and vituperation.

Lasswell describes Mr. A., a typical agitator whom he had studied in great detail:

> A leading characteristic as moralist, socialist, and pacifist has been his truculence in public. Mr. A. speaks rapidly, with great fervor and earnestness, and his discourse is studded with abusive epithets, sarcastic jibes, and cutting insinuations. He confesses that he has taken an unmistakable pleasure in "rubbing the fur the wrong way." He enjoyed nothing better than accepting an invitation to lecture

[43] Sniderman, *Personality and Democratic Politics*, pp. 220–21.

on social and economic subjects before conservative audiences, and scandalizing them.[44]

By contrast, the negotiator is a compromiser. If the agitator feels contempt for the "unprincipled" conduct of the negotiator, the negotiator is baffled by the intransigence of the agitator, who sacrifices immediate gains for abstract principles. The negotiator is more concerned with an acceptable solution to a conflict than a just or perfect solution.

In politics the negotiator is that widely despised figure, the pragmatic or even opportunistic politician. In the extreme case, the pragmatic politician and the agitator hold diametrically opposed views on the importance of current public opinion. The pragmatic politician wants to know what public opinion is, and does not much care what it ought to be. The agitator is interested in what public opinion is only in order to change it to what it ought to be. The pragmatic politician seeks only to respond to public opinion; the agitator tries to make public opinion respond. Wendell Phillips, himself a famous American agitator of the nineteenth century, made an eloquent if somewhat biased contrast between the agitator and the pragmatic politician:

> The reformer is careless of numbers, disregards popularity, and deals only with ideas, conscience, and common sense. He feels, with Copernicus, that as God waited long for an interpreter, so he can wait for his followers. He neither expects nor is overanxious for immediate success. The politician dwells in an everlasting NOW. His Motto is "Success"—his aim, votes. His object is not absolute right, but, like Solon's laws, as much right as the people will sanction. His office is not to instruct public opinion but to represent it. Thus, in England, Cobden, the reformer, created sentiment, and Peel, the politician, stereotyped it into statutes.[45]

By taking current opinion as given, the pragmatic politician is the instrument of current majorities. By taking public opinion as an object to be altered, the agitator helps create future majorities. Both run the fatal risk of being born out of their time. The pragmatic politician born at the wrong time is obedient to opinions today that lead inexorably to disaster tomorrow. Born at the wrong time, the agitator is merely ignored today and, worse yet, forgotten tomorrow.

Wendell Phillips is the prototype of the intelligent agitator; Abraham Lincoln, of the principled politician. Phillips was "an agitator by profession" who "made of agitation an art and a science." He became an abolitionist in the 1830s; after the Civil War he attacked the conciliatory policies of Presi-

[44] Harold Lasswell, *Psychopathology and Politics* (Chicago: University of Chicago Press, 1930), pp. 78–80.

[45] Quoted in Richard Hofstadter, *The American Political Tradition* (New York: Vintage Books; London: Jonathan Cape Ltd., 1954), pp. 138–39. Reprinted by permission of Alfred A. Knopf, Inc., and the Estate of Richard Hofstadter.

dent Johnson, supported Radical Republicans such as Charles Sumner in Congress, demanded the redistribution of landed property in the South, and thus sought to reduce the power of the ex-slaveholders. He sympathized with the First Socialist International, was "a homespun Yankee" socialist, and supported women's rights. It is understandable that a Virginia newspaper once described him as "an infernal machine set to music."[46]

Although Phillips supported Lincoln during the Civil War, the two could hardly have been more different. Lincoln was surely one of the greatest of our pragmatic politicians. If it is hard to imagine Phillips as President, it is difficult to think of Lincoln other than as President. Yet before he entered the White House he had spent most of his mature life acquiring and practicing the arts of the pragmatic politician. At an early age, in Richard Hofstadter's words, he learned "the deliberate and responsible opportunism that was later so characteristic of his statecraft."

> The clue to much that is vital in Lincoln's thought and character lies in the fact that he was thoroughly and completely the politician, by preference and by training. It is difficult to think of any man of comparable stature whose life was so fully absorbed into his political being. Lincoln plunged into politics almost at the beginning of his adult life and was never occupied in any other career except for a brief period when an unfavorable turn in the political situation forced him back to his law practice. His life was one of caucuses and conventions, party circulars and speeches, requests, recommendations, strategems, schemes, and ambitions. "It was the world of politics that he lived," wrote Herndon after his death. "Politics were his life, newspapers his food, and his great ambition his motive power."[47]

It is reasonable to think that popular governments would suffer badly if either the agitator or the negotiator were absent. Negotiators increase the chances for peaceful adjustment of conflicts. Yet short-run peaceful adjustments may take place without considering currently unpopular alternatives, or at the expense of groups who have no advocates and are inadequately represented. The agitator often focuses attention on these neglected alternatives or groups, and, paradoxical as it may seem, may thereby contribute to the discovery of better short-run and long-run solutions. This was Wendell Phillips' view. "Republics," he said, "exist only on the tenure of being constantly agitated. The republic which sinks to sleep, trusting to constitutions and machinery, to politicians and statesmen, for the safety of its liberties, never will have any."[48]

But how can one account for the agitator or the negotiator—the Phillips or the Lincoln? All the factors enumerated to explain democrats and despots

[46] For these and other details of Phillips' life, see "Wendell Phillips: The Patrician as Agitator," Chapter Six in Hofstadter, *ibid.*

[47] *Ibid.*, pp. 95–97. Reprinted by permission of Alfred A. Knopf, Inc.

[48] *Ibid.*, p. 138. Reprinted by permission of Alfred A. Knopf, Inc.

also seem to be required to explain why one person is an agitator and another a negotiator. Personality and character are unquestionably important: The inner needs of the agitator may feed on conflict, those of the negotiator on conciliation. Doubtless the agitator is often *driven* to seek conflict, the negotiator often *impelled* to seek conciliation.

But political culture also plays a part. In some countries, dominant cultural values strongly accent the desirability of obtaining widespread agreement, the virtues of consensus, hence the need to strive for conciliation and compromise, to avoid conflict.[49] As one matures in such a culture, one is gradually socialized in its ways and learns to behave as expected. In some countries, then, people learn at an early age that it is better to negotiate than to agitate.

Yet even in a political culture marked by moderation and conciliation, a particular individual may deviate from the prevailing norms: A person may be driven by inner needs to defy the norms. More important, personal experiences and specific historical situations may alter one's political practices, orientations, even life-style, and conceivably the political culture.

Thus the rise of a new generation of black militants in the 1960s was more than a matter of particular personalities or a political culture: clearly the individual and collective experiences of black people and the historical situation of the 1960s played a decisive part. A substantial amount of evidence suggests that the white political activists of this period were different in some ways from other students, as persons. The radical activists, it appears, differed not only from more conventional students but also from "alienated" students. Yet what crystallized their impulses toward activism was, surely, the historical situation in which they found themselves: widespread opulence and seemingly obsessive consumption confronting poverty, racial conflict, and a highly unpopular war in Viet-Nam sustained by compulsory military service.[50]

Varieties of Pragmatic Politicians. Even pragmatic politicians, of course, cannot be compressed into a single type. James D. Barber has suggested that American politicians in general and Presidents in particular display varying political styles along two dimensions:

> The first baseline in defining Presidential types is *activity-passivity*. How much energy does the man invest in his Presidency? Lyndon Johnson went at his day

[49] Observers have frequently remarked on these qualities in Switzerland and the Scandinavian countries. See, for example, Harry Eckstein's description of Norwegian political norms in *Division and Cohesion in a Democracy: A Study of Norway* (Princeton, N.J.: Princeton University Press, 1966), p. 158 and passim. Putnam found British members of Parliament more likely to emphasize consensus, Italian members more likely to emphasize conflict (*op. cit.*, pp. 101–105, 109–13).

[50] Kenneth Keniston, *Young Radicals* (New York: Harcourt Brace Jovanovich, Inc., 1968), Appendix B., "The Sources of Student Dissent," pp. 297–325, at p. 309.

> like a human cyclone, coming to rest long after the sun went down. Calvin Coolidge often slept eleven hours a night and still needed a nap in the middle of the day. . . . The second baseline is *positive-negative effect* toward one's activity, that is, how he feels about what he does. Relatively speaking, does he seem to experience his political life as happy or sad, enjoyable or discouraging, positive or negative in its main effect.[51]

These two dimensions produce "four basic character patterns long familiar in psychological research." These are the active-positive, the active-negative, the passive-positive, and the passive-negative.

> The first four Presidents, conveniently, ran through the gamut of character types. . . . Washington's dignity, judiciousness, his allover air of reserve and dedication to duty fit the passive-negative or withdrawing type best. . . . John Adams followed, a dour New England Puritan much given to work and worry, an impatient and irrascible man—an active-negative President, a compulsive type. . . . Then came Jefferson . . . Jefferson was clearly active-positive. . . . Madison comes closest to the passive-positive, or compliant type. . . .[52]

How can we explain these different political styles? Barber conjectures that a political style typically emerges relatively early in life, in late adolescence or early adulthood, when in some particular situations one's motives, resources, and opportunities combine to produce what appears to be a successful strategy, which then serves for the rest of one's life. Yet since motives, resources, and opportunities each vary over a wide range, "there is no one 'political man,' no universal pattern of leadership performance,"[53]

Once again, the argument points to the conclusion that individuals who gain power need to be similar to one another only in certain formal respects. In fact, the concrete characteristics of leaders seem to vary a good deal in different cultures, political systems, times, and situations. Leaders have different social origins, resources, skills and personalities.[54] Among

[51] James David Barber, *The Presidential Character: Predicting Performance in the White House* (Englewood Cliffs, N.J.: Prentice-Hall, Inc., 1972) pp. 11–14, and *passim*.

[52] James David Barber, *ibid.* In the *The Lawmakers* (New Haven: Yale University Press, 1965) Barber used the typology to examine Connecticut legislators. For critique, see Alexander George, "Assessing Presidential Character," *World Politics* 26 (January 1974), pp. 234–82 and Erwin C. Hargrove, "Presidential Personality and Revisionist Views of the Presidency," *The American Journal of Political Science* 17 (November 1973),pp. 891–935.

[53] James D. Barber, "Classifying and Predicting Presidential Styles: Two 'Weak' Presidents" *The Journal of Social Issues* 24 (July 1968): 51–80.

[54] This conclusion recently has received further support from the emerging field of "psychohistory," in which an effort is made, usually by psychoanalysts or psychiatrists, to reconstruct the psychological dynamics of an historical figure or, in some cases, an historical movement. Two seminal sources are Alexander L. George and Juliette L. George, *Woodrow Wilson and Colonel House: A Personality Study* (New York: Harper & Row Publishers, Inc., 1956), paperback edition with new preface, (New York: Dover Press, 1964), and Erik H. Erickson, *Young Man Luther* (New York: W. W. Norton & Co., Inc., 1958). For an account and some examples of psychohistory, see *Explorations in Psychohistory; the Wellfleet Papers*, ed. Robert Jay Lifton, with Eric Olson, and with essays by Erik Erikson and Kenneth Keniston (New York: Simon & Schuster, Inc., 1974).

those who have sought and gained power, the range runs from Napoleon Bonaparte, the Corsican upstart, to Winston Churchill, descendant of seven Dukes of Marlborough; from Caesar, the military genius, to Woodrow Wilson, historian, political scientist, and college president; from the detached and reflective Roman emperor Hadrian to the monk Savonarola, the doomed prophet of a Florentine Christian republic; from the regal Elizabeth I to Madam de Pompadour, the witty mistress of Louis XV; from the serene stoicism of philosopher Marcus Aurelius to the neurosis of Hitler and the paranoia of Stalin; from Caligula to Lincoln.

9

POLITICAL EVALUATION

The chances are that like most readers of this book you believe that democracy is better than dictatorship. Is a belief like this exactly equivalent to saying that you like coffee better than tea? If so, your political decisions would not allow for much rational defense. Is this unavoidable? And if your political beliefs are inherently nonrational, isn't it a waste of time trying to act wisely in politics? Isn't a decision based on complete ignorance as justifiable, in the end, as one based on knowledge? If no one knew how to build a foundation and supporting structure strong enough to hold up a house, it would be foolish for anyone to try to live in a house; we would all be better off living in tents instead. Are political beliefs, no matter how carefully constructed, pretty much like a house without foundations or supporting structures strong enough to hold them up?

In considering questions such as these it is obvious that we must move toward a much more explicitly normative orientation than in the earlier chapters, where we were concerned at first with questions of meaning and than mainly with empirical questions. To be sure, because I assumed in those chapters that certain similarities and differences are important, I implicitly used some standards of evaluation. We now explicitly confront the question of how we can reasonable justify such standards, if at all.

THE DECLINE OF POLITICAL PHILOSOPHY

An important place to look for the fundamental foundations and structures of thinking about standards of evaluation is philosophy.[1] For much of this century, however, political philosophy has mainly lived off the capital of the past—the works created by the great political philosophers of previous centuries. Among political scientists, for example, what came to be called "political theory" consisted almost entirely of interpretations of earlier political philosophers. "Political theorists" tended to see their subject as the history, interpretation, and criticism of earlier writings. Because the best political philosophers were not only exceptionally creative but also confronted questions so enduring that we still face them today, political philosophy is rich in works of lasting importance.

In taking on the essential task of transmitting these ideas, however, "political theorists" paid a heavy price: Unlike theorists in other fields—economics, evolutionary biology, and physics, for example—they did not themselves create much new theory. The function of creating political theory moved sharply away from philosophy to empirically oriented political science. Particularly in the period following the Second World War, political scientists with an empirical orientation have produced an explosive growth in empirical political theories that touch on a great variety of crucial subjects—voting behavior, elections, election systems, political parties, political development, the conditions of democracy, the breakdown of democratic regimes, international politics, relations between politics and economics, and so on.

As in the preceding four chapters, the questions these theories deal with are explicitly and primarily empirical and only implicitly normative. Consequently, the creativity of empirical political theory did little to bring about a corresponding creativity in political philosophy and normative theory. Indeed, for reasons we shall now consider, the effect may have been quite the opposite.

Some Causes for the Decline

The absence of great creativity in political philosophy within political science mirrored a more general decline in political philosophy as a whole. The

[1] Some philosophers, undoubtedly a minority, contend that there is nothing about philosophy or philosophers that gives them specially privileged access to truth and thus to knowing about the "foundations" of knowledge, whether of morals, metaphysics, or anything else. In Rorty's view, for example, philosophers can, like the later Wittgenstein, "edify," but they cannot discover special truths about the foundations of knowledge. The aim of philosophers should therefore simply be to contribute to the "conversation" about significant matters, and to keep the conversation going. Richard Rorty, *Philosophy and the Mirror of Nature* (Princeton: Princeton University Press, 1979). In this perspective, another way of describing the decline in political philosophy would be to say that political philosophers failed to keep up their end of the conversation.

distinctive contribution of political philosophy had been its special attention to beliefs about values, norms, standards. Until the nineteenth century, philosophers (like other people) tended to believe that moral ideas could be about as objective and certain as empirical knowledge, because they were ultimately based on divine revelation, nature, or self-evident intuitions. But since the latter part of the nineteenth century and increasingly in the twentieth, many philosophers, and probably large sections of the political stratum in all modern societies, have taken a more subjective view. In the extreme case, as we shall see, they have asserted that no belief about any value standard can ever be rationally justified. In this perspective your saying that you believe freedom is better than slavery is no more objective than your saying that you like coffee better than tea.

The growth of "subjectivist" views is attributable to a number of factors. For one thing, a general decline in religious faith from the eighteenth century onward meant that values could no longer be successfully justified by basing them on divinely revealed religious truths. John Locke (1632–1704), whose work profoundly influenced American thinking at the time of the American Revolution and Constitutional Convention, could argue that "all men are by nature equal" because we are all equally God's children. But two centuries later, his premise was generally believed among philosophers to be too shaky to sustain his assertion. In addition, the triumphant progress of science made nonscientific knowledge look pale by comparison. In fact, a philosophical view that *only* scientific knowledge could lay claim to any objectivity gained ground. The French mathematician and philosopher Auguste Comte (1798–1857) contended that human history progressed through three stages, the religious, the metaphysical, and the scientific. Henceforth, the "positive" sciences would be the foundation for politics, ethics, law, and even religion itself. *Positivism*, as his view was named, reappeared independently in Vienna in the 1920s in an intellectual movement variously called logical positivism, neo positivism, logical empiricism, or scientific empiricism. Although neo-positivism was primarily a philosophical interpretation of the fundamental nature of scientific knowledge, its followers tended to dismiss moral statements as meaningless. In 1936 a young Oxford don, A.J. Ayer, boldly asserted that since, unlike scientific statements, the truth of moral judgments could not be verified, moral statements were devoid of meaning.[2] But if moral assertions are meaningless—or at any rate without rational or (as neo-positivists sometimes said) "cognitive" meaning—then the moral foundations of political philosophy must also be meaningless. And if its moral foundations are inherently meaningless, then political philosophy must be a futile undertaking.

Another current of thought that probably also weakened creative impulses in political philosophy was the view that all philosophical thought (in

[2]A. J. Ayer, *Language, Truth and Logic* (London: Gollancz, 1936; and New York: Holt, Rinehart & Winston, 1973), pp. 226–7,

some versions, all thought of every kind, including the natural sciences) is determined by causes outside the consciousness and beyond the control of those who espouse it. In *deterministic* accounts, the external causes were variously ascribed to a person's particular historical period, culture, class, interests, and psychological developments.[3] If one's philosophical perspective is ultimately nothing more than a by-product of nonrational factors like these, then the attempt to create political philosophy, or for that matter even to discuss it seriously, once again seems pretty unpromising.

Counter-Trends

Objections like these to the possibility that political philosophy could be a rational or even reasonable undertaking did not, however, prove to be lethal. For one thing, intelligent and thoughtful people, including political scientists and philosophers, continued to present and discuss political ideas with the utmost seriousness, and in doing so appeared to believe that their discussions were not purposeless or irrational, no matter what neo-positivists, determinists, historicists, or others might say. Serious concern for political ideas, and thus for some of the fundamental questions of moral and political philosophy, was undoubtedly stimulated by the upheavals of the twentieth century. Two world wars and innumerable smaller ones, the world-wide economic depression of the 1930s, revolution, the breakdown of democracy in several countries, the use and expansion of nuclear weapons, the prospect of nuclear annihilation, the American urban riots of the 1960s, the Vietnam War, Watergate, the near-impeachment and resignation of President Nixon —even among Americans these and other events weakened many of the more comfortable and optimistic beliefs of an earlier time.[4]

[3] The view that human consciousness and actions are fully determined by external factors is generally called *determinism*. An argument for determinism because of psychological factors is presented by the psychologist B. F. Skinner in *Beyond Freedom and Dignity* (New York: Alfred A. Knopf, Inc., 1971). See also *Walden Two* (New York: MacMillan, Inc., 1948) and Finley Carpenter, *The Skinner Primer* (New York: Free Press, 1974). The term *relativism* is often applied to the argument that different factors produce different and even conflicting but equally justifiable ways of understanding, interpreting, and explaining the world among different individuals and different groups. A common form of relativism, particularly among anthropologists, is *cultural* relativism. When applied to morality, such views become *moral relativism*. *Historicism* is a term often applied to historians or others who contend that political (or other) thought can be more or less fully explained and interpreted as a by-product of assumptions grounded in the writer's historical period. Arguments for an historicist view may be found in Quention Skinner, "Meaning and Understanding in the History of Ideas," *History and Theory* 8 (1969): 3–53 and "Some Problems in the Analysis of Political Thought and Action," *Political Theory* 2 (1974): 277–303. A special and important form of historicism has been the *historical determinism* of Marx and his followers. For a recent interpretation, see G. A. Cohen, *Karl Marx: Theory of History* (Princeton: Princeton University Press, 1978).

[4] In a famous aphorism, the philosopher Georg Wilhelm Friedrich Hegel (1770–1831) remarked that the owl of Minerva flies at dusk, by which he meant that philosophy flourished not during the vigorous youth of a civilization when its norms were acted on without much questioning, but during periods of decline when the norms, now no longer seeming appropriate, underwent questioning.

Moreover, the influence of neo-positivism peaked and, as often happens with philosophical movements, rapidly waned. In 1977 A. J. Ayer lamented that he had gone from being a Young Turk to old hat without an intervening period of solid respectability.[5] It became obvious, too, that the philosophical void could not be filled by purely deterministic accounts.[6]

Analysis of Meaning

Some philosophers, particularly in English-speaking countries, came to believe that a satisfactory foundation for reasoning about the normative questions in political philosophy might be found in *language*, by analyzing the *meaning* we give to words and concepts in ordinary usage. The analysis of meanings in moral and political evaluation is strongly influenced by the later work of the philosopher Ludwig Wittgenstein (1889–1951)[7]. In general, "analytic" or "linguistic" philosophy seeks the meaning of terms as these are actually used in ordinary, nonphilosophical language. As a result of reflecting on how we express our meaning when we wish to indicate moral and evaluative judgments, as distinguished from judgments about matters in the domain of empirical science, some writers have concluded that language is in effect divided into different "regions." The languages of different "regions" deal with different matters. The language of one region is often inappropriate and confusing when it is applied to matters requiring a rather different sort of language.

One such region, it has been argued, is moral discourse.[8] To rely exclusively on the language of the empirical sciences to explore the domain of moral discourse (as, it is argued, some noncognitivists propose to do) is fundamentally as absurd as using the language of physics or chemistry in order to discuss the esthetic qualities of a painting. One aim of the approach—with some practitioners, the exclusive aim—is to enrich and clarify moral discourse and political evaluation by heightening our understanding of the

[5] Quoted in Brian Barry, "And Who is My Neighbor?" *The Yale Law Journal*, 88:629 (1979), 629–58, at p. 631, from Ayer's autobiography, *A Part of My Life* (London: Oxford Univ. Press, 1977), pp. 294–95.

[6] As Deborah Baumgold remarks of historicism, "Not surprisingly, the historicist approach . . . tends to dissolve the political interest of the classic texts." Her essay, "Political Commentary on the History of Political Theory," *American Political Science Review*, 75:4 (December 1981), 928–40, is a useful description and critique of several recent approaches to political philosophy.

[7] Wittgenstein's later work is somewhat at odds with his earlier work, which strongly influenced logical positivism. For an account of his work, see David Pears, *Ludwig Wittgenstein* (New York: The Viking Press, 1969, 1970).

[8] Hanna Fenichel Pitkin, *Wittgenstein and Justice* (Berkeley: University of California Press, 1972). Although less directly influenced by Wittgenstein, Brian Barry, *Political Argument* (New York: Humanities Press, Inc., 1967) also stresses and exemplifies the possibilities of clarifying political judgments through (in part) the meticulous analysis of meaning. Wittgenstein's work also plays an important role in Peter Winch's critique of the social sciences, *The Idea of a Social Science and its Relation to Philosophy* (New York: Humanities Press, 1958).

language we use when we discuss moral questions, as practically everybody does.

As an approach to the restoration of moral and political philosophy, however, linguistic analysis soon revealed its own shortcomings. Perhaps the most important was its failure to show convincingly how the analysis of meaning could avoid what earlier philosophers had called the *naturalistic fallacy*: the attempt to derive a statement about what we *ought* to do from statements about what *is*. Even if it were possible to show what we mean by the term "justice" in certain contexts, it would not appear to follow that we *ought* to act justly. Moreover, no analytic philosopher actually produced a work in political philosophy so powerful and convincing as to demonstrate the success of the approach. Finally, analyzing the meaning of terms often became so tedious, trivial, or arcane that no one except professional philosophers could follow the discussion, or cared to.[9]

REVIVAL

In 1971, John Rawls, a Harvard philosopher, published his long-awaited *A Theory of Justice.*[10] His work was immediately recognized in English-speaking countries as a fundamental contribution ot political philosophy. It stimulated an unprecedented outpouring of articles, even entire books, interpreting, supporting, or, as is usual among scholars, attacking Rawls's argument.[11] Some critics who rejected his theory or important parts of it nonetheless used it as a point of departure to develop alternate views. Throughout the following decade works appeared almost annually that grappled directly with some major question in political philosophy and attempted to set forth a solution. It is too early to say whether all this signifies a long-run revival in political philosophy or is only a blip on the radar screen of intellectual history. Meanwhile, however, the normative orientation has become a

[9] "So far has the pendulum swung to the other extreme that I cannot remember when I last read a discussion about the criteria for a good cactus or an extra-fancy apple". Barry, "And Who is My Neighbor", p. 632.

[10] John Rawls, *A Theory of Justice* (Cambridge: Harvard University Press 1971). In emphasizing Rawls, I do some injustice to other writers, particularly European philosophers or those, like the late Hannah Arendt, trained in the European tradition of political philosophy, which tends to be more historical and less disposed to confront normative issues directly than has been usual in English political thought since Hobbes and Locke. Thus in this chapter I have ignored the influence in continental Europe, England, and the United States of the German philosopher Jürgen Habermas, whose important works have also all appeared since 1970. For a detailed analysis, see Thomas McCarthy, *The Critical Theory of Jürgen Habermas* (Cambridge, Mass.: MIT Press, 1978). A list of his works available in English is on p. 444.

[11] For example, Brian Barry, *The Liberal Theory of Justice* (Oxford: Clarendon Press, 1973); and Robert Paul Wolff, *Understanding Rawls* (Princeton: Princeton University Press, 1977). See also the articles devoted to Rawls in *The American Political Science Review*, 69:2 (June 1975).

rapidly expanding frontier of political science, just as empirical analysis has become earlier. Fortunately, the revival of political philosophy need not impede the continuing growth of empirical analysis, and may even strengthen it by suggesting criteria that will help empirical investigators to judge the relative importance of questions they might undertake to study.

Rawls's Argument

While there is insufficient space in this slender volume to describe these recent developments in normative theory,[12] something of its flavor can perhaps be conveyed by a brief examination of three aspects of *A Theory of Justice*. Rawls's argument reflects his belief in the validity of one of two fundamental *types* of moral reasoning. He proposes a *procedure* for arriving at principles of this type. And he presents two *principles of justice* that he claims to justify by means of the procedure.

Two Types of Moral Reasoning. One common form of moral reasoning is based exclusively on an estimate of the net sum of value of alternative *consequences*, arrived at by summing up the gains and losses for each person: as, for example, in the principle that the best rule of public policy is to seek "the greatest good of the greatest number." For obvious reasons this kind of moral reasoning is called *consequentialist*. The consequences must be evaluated, of course, against some standard of what is good or desirable. Familiar standards are happiness, pleasure, satisfaction, utility, and the like. An argument using standards like these is generally called *utilitarian*. Utilitarians typically hold that the best policy is one that *maximizes* some chosen value—happiness, utility, or whatever.[13] From its inception, modern economics has taken the validity of utilitarian reasoning for granted, even though the concept of utility in economics has become so abstract and disembodied that it is now only a ghostly wraith of its earlier robust life in the form of happiness or pleasure. Many of our judgments about public policies are based on utilitarian considerations. We try to estimate the gains and costs to different persons or groups in society and arrive at a judgment favoring the

[12] An excellent critical analysis of the contributions of Rawls, Kant, Aristotle, and many others, together with a presentation of his own theory of justice, is William A. Galston, *Justice and the Human Good* (Chicago: University of Chicago Press, 1980).

[13] One problem in maximizing schemes, and thus in utilitarianism, is whether to maximize the total sum of value, or the average. Classical utilitarians specified that the total sum of value ought to be maximized. But suppose a country could choose between (1) doubling its population and increasing GNP by 20% or (2) keeping both population and GNP the same. Maximizing the total sum would require the first policy, even though the average person's share would be reduced by 60%. Modern utilitarians have therefore advocated maximizing average utility, which would lead to the second policy. See the discussion in Rawls, pp. 161ff. Of course GNP is not necessarily equivalent to happiness, pleasure, satisfaction, utility, or any other reasonable standard of goodness. But that points to another problem of utilitarianism: how to estimate the relative value of the alternatives.

policy with the greatest net gain for the entire aggregate. In fact, it is difficult to see how you could make a sensible judgment about public policies if you were absolutely forbidden to employ utilitarian reasoning.

In his theory of justice, however, Rawls explicitly rejects utilitarian reasoning.[14] Instead, he grounds his theory in another familiar notion: Most of us believe some things are right, good, or just even though they might not, for example, produce the greatest happiness for the greatest number. Thus, if people have inalienable, inviolable, natural rights, then such a right should never be overriden by a mere summing up of the net utility, pleasure, or happiness of others. If people have an inviolable right to fair trial, they ought not to be deprived of that right simply because of the pleasure that convicting them might give to others, whether an aroused mob in search of a victim for lynching, a legislature wanting to ensure the conviction of an unpopular group of dissenters, or, for that matter, a majority of citizens. As Rawls says, "Justice denies that the loss of freedom for some is made right by a greater good shared by others."[15] In contrast to utilitarian reasoning, Rawls's insistence on the absolute priority of certain principles of justice reflects what Barry calls "absolutism"[16] and Rawls, "deontological" moral theory.[17]

Rawls was hardly the first to criticize utilitarian reasoning. If he made a bigger splash in political philosophy than previous critics, it was probably because he presented both a procedure for justifying absolute principles and two relatively specific principles to boot.

Rawls's Procedure. A central difficulty in moral reasoning is how to arrive at principles that can reasonably claim to be *general* or even *universal*. Principles based only on your own self-interest will hardly be persuasive to anyone whose interests are opposed to yours. Rawl's procedure is intended to overcome this difficulty.

He invites you to imagine yourselves with others attempting to arrive at an original agreement, a social contract, embodying the principles of justice

[14] Rawls, *Theory of Justice*, pp. 22–27 and 150–92.

[15] Ibid., p. 28.

[16] Barry, "And Who is My Neighbor?", *op. cit.* p. 630.

[17] Rawls defines a deontological theory as "one that either does not specify the good independently from the right, or does not interpret the right as maximizing the good." That is, in a deontological theory either (1) what is best is not some separate end like happiness but simply bringing about what is *right*, such as justice, irrespective of other ends; or (2) what is best is not determined by maximizing the attainment of some desirable end like happiness but is an absolute requirement, regardless of the total sum of, say, happiness, that might result. In rejecting utilitarianism, Rawls does not reject consequentialist arguments in general. Deontological theories such as his do not "characterize the rightness of institutions and acts independently from their consequences. All ethical doctrines worth our attention take consequences into account in judging rightness. One which did not would simply be irrational, 'crazy'" (*Theory of Justice* p. 30). His point is that while justice obviously requires us to take consequences into account—for example, whether a fair trail is or is not a consequence of certain procedures—justice is not a matter of a net sum of individual gains and losses but is an absolute right.

for the basic structure of your society. The principles are to be what you as a free and rational person, concerned to further your own interests, would accept in an initial position of equality with the others. That is, you and others are presumed to have the the same rights in choosing principles; each of you can make proposals, submit reasons for their acceptance, and so on. In one of his most ingenious and controversial moves, however, Rawls proposes that you imagine yourself to be in a hypothetical situation behind "a veil of ignorance" as to your own concrete, personal, individual interests. You are to choose rules of justice as if you don't know for sure what your own situation in the new society is going to be: whether you will be advantaged or disadvantaged, rich or poor, weak or powerful, smart or slow, and so on. In this "original position," what fundamental rules would you want to put into your social contract and subsequently have reflected in your Constitution?[18] Because of your uncertainty, he argues, you will want to make sure that the rules will prevent you from being treated too severely if you should turn out to be one of the less-advantaged persons in your society. And after all, how can you be sure what the future may bring, not only for you but for other members of your family—for your children?

Two Principles of Justice. In these circumstances, Rawls contends, you would adopt the following general principles of justice:

> All social values—liberty and opportunity, income and wealth, and the bases of self-respect—are to be distributed equally unless an unequal distribution of any, or all, of these values is to everyone's advantage.[19]

Rawls unpacks from this general principle two principles of justice: The first guarantees full equality of political rights as citizens in a democratic order. The second guarantees fair (though not necessarily perfectly equal) treatment in the distribution of social and economic values.

First, then, each person is to have an equal right to the most extensive basic liberty compatible with a similar liberty for others.

> The basic liberties of citizens are, roughly speaking, political liberty (the right to vote and to be eligible for public office) together with freedom of speech and assembly; liberty of conscience and freedom of thought; freedom of the person, along with the right to hold (personal) property; and freedom from arbitrary arrest and seizure as defined by the concept of the rule of law. These liberties are all required to be equal by the first principle, since citizens of a just society are to have the same basic rights.[20]

[18] *Ibid.*, pp. 11–22. I have ignored two other important and highly controversial aspects of Rawls' procedures, his notion of reflective equilibrium (pp. 48–51), briefly discussed below in footnote 25. p. 132 and his adoption of a maximin strategy (pp. 151–56).

[19] *Ibid.*, p. 62.

[20] *Ibid.*, p. 62.

Thus Rawls's first principle establishes the fundamental rights of citizenship in a liberal democratic political order. And it takes absolute priority over the second principle: "A departure from the institutions of equal liberty required by the first principle cannot be justified by, or compensated for, by greater social and economic advantages."[21]

Nonetheless, Rawls's second principle goes well beyond prevailing policies in democratic countries: Social and economic inequalities are not to be permitted except under two conditions: the inequalities are to the benefit of *everyone* in the society, and *everyone* has an equal opportunity to seek the positions to which unequal rewards are attached.[22] Thus, under the second principle, inequalities in wealth and income could not be justified as consequences of the right to property or differences in ability, talents, or work. Income and wealth would have to be distributed equally among citizens unless it could be shown that inequality would make everyone better off—perhaps by strengthening incentives and output so that the income of *everyone* would rise. Clearly the application of Rawls's two principles of justice to the United States would require a profound change in public policy.

SOME IMPLICATIONS

Although such a brief discussion necessarily does an injustice to Rawls's argument, it does suggest several conclusions.

1. The Progress of Science Has Not Eliminated Political Philosophy

It is obvious, to begin with, that the view of Comte mentioned earlier and implicitly shared by some neo-positivists—that strictly scientific analysis would replace moral and political philosophy—has simply not been borne out. Even during the dog days when Anglo-American political philosophy was in the doldrums, serious discussion did take place and attempts were made to move the discussion forward by using new methods, such as the analysis of meaning practiced in analytic philosophy. In fact, probably one reason for the extraordinary attention paid to *A Theory of Justice* is that it loomed up like an oasis in the desert, and to thirsty social theorists craving a refreshing discussion, it was uncommonly welcome.

There is no evident reason why an empirical or scientific orientation need be fundamentally at odds with a normative orientation. Each would enrich the other. Without the mapping of reality produced by empirically

[21] *Ibid.*, p. 61. See also his justification for the priority of liberty, pp. 541ff.
[22] *Ibid.*, pp. 60–61 and 302–3.

oriented analysis, political philosophy can easily become irrelevant or simply silly. Without concern for some of the fundamental questions typically posed by political philosophers, whether ancient or contemporary, empirical analysis runs the risk of degenerating into triviality.

2. Meaningful Discussion of Moral Questions Does Take Place

If hundreds of otherwise rational scholars have seriously discussed, interpreted, analyzed, argued with, and accepted or rejected, in whole or in part, *A Theory of Justice*, then it seems rather arbitrary and dogmatic to contend that a theory like Rawls's is meaningless, necessarily lacks "cognitive" meaning, is inherently incapable of rational justification, and thus lies outside the bounds of reasoned discussion. For it is perfectly obvious that rational and reasonable people *do* find Rawls's theory meaningful. To be sure, they may not find it meaningful in the way that a physicist would find the statement, "Although quarks are a fundamental constituent of protons, they can neither exist in isolation nor be observed," meaningful. Of course, a theory like Rawls's may be wrong. But in principle, so might any empirical proposition, including the one about quarks.

3. Political Philosophy is Inescapably Controversial

Nonetheless, it is extremely unlikely that any philosophical theory will ever gain the degree of consensus among experts that often develops around certain scientific theories. From its very beginnings, statements and theories in political philosophy have been highly controversial. Socrates thrived on controversy, and Aristotle disagreed fundamentally with his teacher Plato, Socrates' most famous pupil. As I have already suggested, one of the remarkable achievements of *A Theory of Justice* is the amount of controversy it triggered. Critics have attacked virtually every part of Rawls's theory. Among other objections, critics contend that:

- It is unreasonable to give absolute priority to principles of justice over all utilitarian considerations.
- The veil of ignorance is too artificial, since you cannot reasonably be expected to choose principles in complete ignorance of your own future prospects.
- It is not necessarily rational to be as cautious in the face of uncertainty as Rawls believes. If you would like to gamble on your chances of coming out on top, you might reasonably want rules that would permit much greater inequality than do Rawls's two principles.
- To give absolute priority to political rights over social and economic rights is not necessarily a reasonable trade-off, except perhaps in wealthy countries.[23]

[23] Rawls assumes a "condition of moderate scarcity" in which "natural and other resources are not so abundant that schemes of cooperation become superfluous, nor are conditions so harsh

- The second principle would forbid adopting any policy under which the worst-off would gain nothing, or suffer an ever-so-slight loss, even if many slightly better-off people would gain a great deal. This seems utterly unreasonable.
- And so on.

Since the past does not invariably foretell the future, the fact that political philosophy has been extremely controversial from time of Socrates, through Rawls's time, to yesterday does not guarantee that it will always be so. Adherents to a particular philosophy or ideology often seem to believe that their own views are so reasonable that no reasonable person could, on understanding them, disagree. Consequently the hope never dies that a particular philosophical or ideological perspective—usually one's own, of course—will in time gain universal endorsement.

Yet the fact that the historical record is one of disagreement and controversy is surely no accident. There are, in fact, powerful reasons for believing that no specific political philosophy is ever likely to command general agreement among political philosophers, social theorists, political leaders, ideologues, activists, and ordinary citizens—at least in places where opportunities exist for relatively free discussion.

How Decide the Truth of Philosophical Theories? For one thing, to prescribe how the truth of a philosophical theory is to be decided is itself a difficult, highly controversial question. To be sure, in the natural sciences the relations among theory, experiment, and reality are far more complex than is commonly supposed, particularly, perhaps, in the rapidly expanding field of particle physics.[24] Yet nature does have its ways—sometimes gentle, sometimes brutal—of reminding theorists of what it will tolerate as valid theoretical descriptions about it. But whether nature, or any other reality, imposes limits on the truth of moral theories, and if so how and what, are themselves sharply debated issues.[25] It is not only that moral theories

---

that fruitful ventures must inevitably break down" (p. 127, 257). Since it is unlikely that "fruitful ventures must *inevitably* break down" in any society, literally interpreted Rawls's condition of moderate scarcity would exist even in Bangladesh, and thus practically everywhere in the world. Clearly, however, Rawls does not mean his words to be interpreted literally at this point. Only as he approaches the end of his long book does Rawls explain *why* he assigns priority to liberty: "[A]s the conditions of civilization improve, the marginal significance for our own good of further economic and social advantages diminishes relative to the interests of liberty. . ." because "as the general level of well-being rises. . only the less urgent wants remain to be met by further advances. " while the advantages of liberty increase (pp. 542–543).

[24] For an extreme example, see Bernard d'Espagnat, "The Quantum Theory and Reality," *Scientific American*, Vol. 241 pp. 158–81 (November, 1979). The article is summarized as follows: "The doctrine that the world is made up of objects whose existence is independent of human consciousness turns out to be in conflict with quantum mechanics and with facts established by experiment" (p. 158).

[25] Thus Rawls advances "the notion of reflective equilibrium" as a way of testing the validity of a moral philosophy. What he means is unclear. He proposes that we reflect about alternative conceptions in a considered way, under conditions in which we are not "influenced by an excessive

themselves are highly controversial. It is as if physicists could not agree whether protons exist until they settled the philosophical question as to whether anything exists "out there" and how we can possibly know about it if it does.

Ultimate Grounds? An important reason for disagreement on how we should decide about the truth of moral judgments is that people disagree about the ultimate grounds on which moral judgments are to be justified. These grounds include divine revelation, as in the Ten Commandments; authority, as in authoritatively received accounts of divine revelations, such as the Bible or the Koran, and subsequent interpretations of these accounts given by rabbis, priests, religious leaders, mullahs, monks, etc.; awareness produced by holistic or mystical union with the cosmos in an extraordinary state of consciousness; intuition; feelings; personal or general experiences; the "common sense of mankind"; and reason. Someone who justifies a moral judgment on one of these grounds is not likely to convince you of its validity if you happen to believe such judgments can be justified only on some different ground.

Meaning of Key Concepts? Because key terms in philosophical theory often refer to extremely complex concepts, language itself is frequently a barrier to agreement. Ambiguities of meaning may contribute to flatly contradictory understandings and to support for fundamentally conflicting policies. As an example, consider a concept that has played a central role in veiws about democracy and justice from Plato and Aristotle to Rawls and his critics: equality. What do we mean by equality?

> "Equality is the simplest and most abstract of notions," Douglas Rae has written, "yet the practices of the world are irremediably concrete and complex. How, imaginably, could the former govern the latter? It cannot. We are always confronted with more than one practical meaning for equality and equality itself cannot provide a basis for choosing among them."[26]

We cannot think clearly about equality, Rae contends, without a "grammar of equality" that unpacks its various and often contradictory meanings. If you are not aware of these different meanings, you can easily choose and justify contradictory policies, all in the name of equality. Although there is insufficient space here to present Rae's grammer in full. I want to mention two striking examples of meanings that are fundamentally contradictory. *Equality of*

---

attention to our own interests." Under these conditions you imaginatively test out the alternative conceptions against your "sense of justice," modify your original judgments, and finally arrive at a judgment that best fits your own sense of justice (p. 48ff.). The possibility that you may end up where you started, but with a more firmly rationalized position, is hardly to be dismissed.

[26] Douglas Rae, *Equalities* (Cambridge: Harvard University Press. 1981). p. 150.

Opportunity, Rae points out, is not one thing, it is two very different things. Equal opportunity may be either

- *Prospect-regarding*—each person has the same *probability* of attaining a given goal, such as a job or admission to a medical school; or
- *Means-regarding*—each person has the same *means* for attaining a given goal.

If you wanted to create the first kind of equal opportunity, you would try to ensure that everyone had an equal chance to get the job or the slot in medical school, no matter what their means or resources might be. If you wanted to create the second, you would try to ensure that everyone had the same means, instruments, resources, or capabilities for getting there. But as Rae points out:

> Given strictly unequal talents, every policy of means-regarding equal opportunity must violate equality of prospects, and every prospect-regarding equal opportunity must violate equality of means.[27]

You simply cannot have it both ways.

Another fundamental conflict among policies arises because equality may be either:

1. *Lot-regarding*—people are awarded identical kinds of things, or lots, or portions, or the like.
2. *Person-regarding*—different persons are awarded things that are of equal value to each person, though they may not be identical in quantity.

Lot-regarding equality means identical treatment for everyone. It is lot-regarding equality to award one vote to each citizen, guarantee everyone twelve years of free schooling, or ensure that everyone between the ages of 18 and 30 has an exactly equal chance to be drafted for military service. But, as Rae points out, draftees would also receive lot-regarding equality if they were all issued size 8-D boots. Obviously it would be fairer—and much more sensible all around—not to issue identical boots to everyone but to issue each person boots that fit. This is person-regarding equality. A commonly used example is this: Suppose you have healthy kidneys and your friend, who does not, will die without regular and expensive dialysis. Identical treatment, or lot-regarding equality, would require either that you both receive dialysis, or that neither does. Obviously either policy is foolish, and the second would be deadly for your friend. In this case, a policy based on person-regarding equality would make it possible for your friend to receive dialysis, while you would not get any treatment at all.[28]

[27] *Ibid.*, pp. 64–69. Difficulties in the idea of equal opportunity are also discussed in John H. Schaar, "Equality of Opportunity, and Beyond" in J. Roland Pennock and John W. Chapman, eds. *Equality (Nomos IX)*. New York: Atherton Press, 1967), pp. 228–249.

[28] Cf. the discussion in Rae, Chapter 5, pp. 82–103.

A lot-regarding policy is usually much easier to specify and apply because all you need to do is to hand out identical bundles of things—dollars, votes, chances of being drafted, or whatnot. You need only to judge whether two or more piles of things are of equal magnitude. You do not need to arrange things into heaps that may vary in size in order to have the same value for different people. The problem is, then, that although a policy based on lot-regarding equality would be easier to apply, it would often be grossly unfair, while a policy of person-regarding equality, though sometimes much fairer, would also be more difficult to apply because you must somehow determine the value things have for different persons. You might easily be tempted therefore to go along with lot-regarding equality (which, after all, is sometimes fair) or to abandon the idea of equality altogether. But if you choose the first, you will often bring about extreme injustice, while if you choose the second, you will simply be throwing in the towel.

An Inescapable Plurality of Modern Perspectives? It should not be surprising, then, that political and moral philosophy is so controversial. Althouth many writers, like Rawls, appear to believe that reasonable human beings should be able to reach agreement, some philosophers contend that the domain of value contains a diversity of particular values, such as freedom, equality, love, and courage, that cannot necessarily be melded into a single harmonious system. The most eminent exponent of this view was the American psychologist and philosopher, William James (1842–1910), who contended that the universe of values is inescapably pluralistic.[29] To use contemporary jargon, if the universe of values is pluralistic, then there are bound to be trade-offs among conflicting values.

More recently, Thomas Nagel has argued that values conflicts also arise because different *systems* of value may specify different courses of concrete action. He describes "five fundamental types of value that give rise to basic conflict." These are specific obligations, of the kind you have to your friends and family (whose life should you first try to save in an emergency?); utility, which we encountered earlier as the most prominent form of consequentialism; general or universal rights, as in Rawls; perfectionist values like freedom, love, dignity, respect, justice, and so on; and your commitment to carrying out your own life plans—being the person you are and want to be. These sometimes lay down conflicting requirements for your actions and policies, and in Nagel's view they are so fundamentally different that "no single, reductive method or a clear set of priorities" exists for settling conflicts among them."[30]

[29] William James, *A Pluralistic Universe* (New York: Longman, Inc., 1909).

[30] Thomas Nagel, "The Fragmentation of Value," in *Mortal Questions* (Cambridge: Cambridge University Press, 1979), pp. 128–41. James S. Fishkin, in *The Limits of Obligation* (New Haven: Yale University Press, 1982) contends that "our common ethical assumptions, which work well enough at the small scale, break down when they are applied to large enough numbers" (p. 3). He shows that when applied on a large scale, the common assumption of moral reasoning that we

Extraneous Influences on Moral Thinking? So far I have largely ignored the possible effects of various "extraneous" influences on our moral judgments. But we cannot ignore the force of our own particular interests, our ideological commitments, the special influences of our own culture, environment, and historical period, and loyalties that, though perhaps nonrational, are necessary to the continuing existence of any community.[31] You cannot make moral judgments or adopt a political philosophy, or for that matter create one, in a complete personal, social, and historical vacuum.

DIVERSITY, CONFLICTS, REGIMES

Conflict over values—and so over political philosophies—appears to be unavoidable. That is a problem both for a person and for a political system.

As I said at the beginning of this chapter, no person can altogether avoid employing standards of value in making judgments. To say that you will refuse to make any judgments unless you can be absolutely certain about the ultimate validity of your own values is itself a moral judgment—one based, I should think, on a highly uncertain standard of value, and a bit shabby, to boot. You can, however, attempt to arrive at judgments responsibly, by trying to understand the significance and consequences of the alternatives available. Of course, if you prefer, you can also choose to act irresponsibly.

Conflicting views about values and the policies they might justify also pose problems for a political system. How should such conflicts be dealt with, and what institutions are best for dealing with them? To answer these questions responsibly would require you to circle back through the topics taken up in previous chapters: the forms of influence, your evaluation of coercion and

---

all have some *general* or universal obligations conflicts with two other common assumptions about moral obligations: (1) that there should be a cut-off for heroism—certain levels of sacrifice cannot morally be required of any given individual; and (2) that there is a robust zone of indifference—a substantial proportion of any person's activities fall within a zone where free personal choice is morally permissible (that is, we aren't required to do *everything* we do because of a moral obligation, which would make life a living hell).

[31] For the contrary view that among all peoples, irrespective of culture, history and so on, moral understanding, like language, spatial and temporal relations, and number, develops through certain definite *stages*, see the work of the psychologist Lawrence Kohlberg, in particular, *The Philosophy of Moral Development, Moral Stages and the Idea of Justice* (San Francisco: Harper & Row Publishers, Inc., 1981). Although most people may not reach the sixth and highest stage of universal ethical principles, everyone, Kohlberg contends, moves throuth the *same* stages. These begin with simply obeying rules to avoid punishment; develop to a second stage of conforming to obtain rewards, have favors returned, and so on; up to stage 5, seeing right action in terms of individual rights agreed on by the whole society; and finally, to stage 6, choosing ethical principles that are logically comprehensive, universal, and consistent, such as the Golden Rule or Kant's Categorical Imperative. For his summary of the stages, see pp. 17–20. Needless to say, the validity of Kohlberg's empirical theory is itself controversial.

rational persuasion, the significance of differences in political regimes, the institutions of polyarchy, its requirements and prospects, and even the political nature of human beings. Your answer would constitute your moral philosophy.

10

CHOOSING POLICIES: STRATEGIES OF INQUIRY AND DECISION

Choosing a policy implies that you possess both normative standards and empirical judgments. For when you choose a policy, you are trying to move toward some goal that you believe is desirable, and you are therefore compelled to make judgments about the possible ways of reaching that goal and how easy or difficult each might be. A good policy is a path to the best situation you can reach at a cost you think it worthwhile to pay.

For reasons that previous chapters make evident, the act of adopting a policy, particularly an important policy, is nearly always surrounded by a cloud of uncertainty. We are uncertain as to matters of fact: If we elect X, what will he actually do in office? Are the policies I want more likely to be achieved through a third party than through one of the major parties? Is the society I desire more likely to be fostered by increasing participation in politics? If so, what can I do to expand participation? Would the use of violence for specific ends I favor significantly increase the chances of a repressive reaction?

We are often uncertain, too, as to matters of value: If decentralization, which I favor, leads to less racial integration, which I also favor, where do I stand? Is coercive violence, which I regard as intrinsically evil, ever justified—as in the American Revolution or the Civil War? If not, am I simply permitting coercive violence by others? If so, in what circumstances? When, if ever, is intolerance of opinion or advocacy justified in a democracy?

Uncertainty over the answers to questions like these, and there are thousands of such questions, seems to be inherent in political life. What strategies of inquiry help to improve the quality of one's political decisions amid the inevitable uncertainties?

Strategies of Pure Science. There is a long-enduring and apparently irrepressible hope among students of politics that a choice among different political alternatives can be based on a pure science of politics. In earlier times, this pure science was to have included not only the factual or empirical elements, as in physics or chemistry, but also the normative or evaluational elements. In this century, however, as the term "science" increasingly has come to mean *empirical* science, the aspiration toward a pure science of politics has come to mean an empirical science of politics. According to this view, an empirical science of politics would be concerned exclusively with the validity of the factual or empirical elements. To be sure, its knowledge would be applied in action; but the validity of the ends, goals, or values sought in action would, as such, lie outside the domain of the pure science.

Some advocates of a pure science of politics share the belief of certain positivists mentioned in the last chapter that although there are scientific procedures for establishing the objective validity of empirical propositions, no procedures exist for determining the objective truth or falsity of a statement asserting that something is good or valuable. But the idea of a pure science of politics is not necessarily opposed by those who believe it is possible to arrive at objective standards of value. After all, one who believes in the value of health would probably want an empirical science of medicine that a doctor might use to cure a sick patient. So, too, one who believes that some form of equality, for example, is objectively better than inequality might advocate an empirical science of politics that would, among other things, provide reliable scientific knowledge about the conditions that facilitate or hinder attaining this equality.

Is a pure science of politics possible or desirable? Like all the other questions touched on in this chapter, this too is vigorously contested. Lack of space prevents us from exploring the major issues here.[1] Nonetheless, if only to illustrate the complexities of the argument, it may be useful to take a brief look at several of the issues.

Can Political Phenomena Be Measured? As everyone knows, discoveries in the natural sciences have been greatly aided by possibilities of measure-

[1] Cf. J. Donald Moon, "The Logic of Political Inquiry: A Synthesis of Opposed Perspectives," in *The Handbook of Political Science*, ed. Fred I. Greenstein and Nelson W. Polsby (Reading, Mass.: Addison-Wesley Publishing Co., Inc., 1975). Further references are found on p. 148.

ment. Nature, it has been said, loves quantity. One key subject of dispute is the extent to which valid and reliable measures, comparable to those used in the natural sciences, can be developed for political phenomena.

In politics as elsewhere, it is an enormous and obvious advantage to be able to measure differences. Suppose one is wrestling with the question of what political system is best. One might then wish to know what difference it makes whether a system is a polyarchy or one of the many alternatives to polyarchy.

Consider the familiar way of analyzing experience symbolized in Figure 10–1. The paradigm is commonplace not only in the natural sciences, in medicine, and in the social and behavioral sciences but also in everyday life. In Chapter 5, we applied it to political systems; we can also apply it to political evaluation. Suppose, for example, that differences in "coercion," "conflict," or "personal freedom" are thought to be important. We may then want to know whether differences in characteristics of political systems (II) have consequences for "coercion," "conflict," or "personal freedom" (I). If they do, then we also may want to know what conditions (III) are likely to bring about or prevent the development of a "freedom-enhancing" system, or a "minimal-coercion" system, or a "peaceful-settlement" system. This kind of thinking is *causal analysis*, the attempt to understand causes. In politics, as in medicine, one wants to understand causes in order to obtain desired results, such as enhanced freedom, greater equality, more security, less coercion, greater social peace, or other goals.

But how can we find out what changes in conditions (III) produce variations in systems (II), which in turn lead to differences in consequences (I)? For self-evident reasons, politics largely excludes the possibility of experimentation in a strict sense. Fortunately, however, good logical approximations to experimentation can be made by the application of rather powerful quantitative methods—provided the data are in quantitative form. One recent innovation in political analysis—both a cause and an effect of the flood of data—is a vigorous attempt to develop ways of measuring political phenomena to provide quantitative and not merely qualitative data bearing on relevant differences.

Some of the older skepticism about quantitative data was a product of

FIGURE 10–1 Analyzing Experience: A Common Paradigm

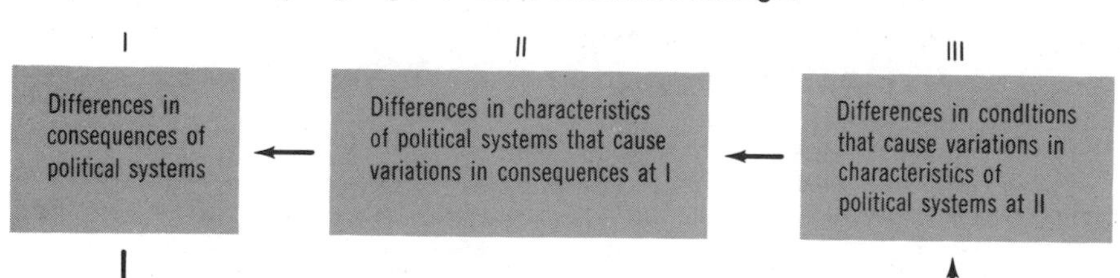

rather unsophisticated ideas about measurement. Most people think of "measurement" only in terms of what specialists on measurement call *interval*-measures, like those used for height, weight, population, area, and so on. Although interval-measures are used for some phenomena relevant to differences in political systems—rates of voter turnout in elections, for example—most political phenomena are subject at best only to *ordinal* measurement, that is, a ranking according to "more," "equal," or "less." Fortunately, ranking or ordinal measurement also allows powerful quantitative methods to be used on data.

One advantage of quantitative data, then, is that they greatly facilitate causal analysis. A second advantage is that quantitative data can be much more efficiently analyzed than qualitative data, particularly with the aid of computers. Quantitative methods thus offer a possible way of coping with the flood of data about political systems that now threatens to inundate us. Although the prospect seems slight that quantitative methods will ever entirely displace the more familiar methods of qualitative analysis, it is hardly open to doubt that in the future, political analysis will make far more use of quantitative data and methods than it has in the past.[2]

When Does a Difference "Make a Difference"? When is a difference trivial and when does it matter? One can rapidly traverse a very small circle right back to the starting point: A difference matters if one thinks that directly or indirectly it has large enough consequences for one's values. Large enough for what? Large enough to matter.

In political controversy it is not always possible to break out of this circle. What is important to one observer sometimes seems utterly trivial to another. To many an American the differences between "democracy" as practiced in the United States and "socialist democracy" as practiced in the Soviet Union are highly important. To an anarchist, the differences might seem to be trivial variations in two oppressively authoritarian systems.

If disagreement as to whether a difference is trivial or important cannot *always* be settled, dispute of this kind *sometimes* can be profitably bypassed. For in practice, many people do share similar views about the relative importance of certain differences. Moreover, a solution satisfactory to all can sometimes be obtained by an analysis that takes into account *all* the differences thought to be relevant. An explanation of why different modern societies develop such varying political systems as inclusive polyarchies, competitive oligarchies, conservative authoritarian regimes, and modernizing dictatorships would be important to advocates of each type of system. These considerations suggest an obvious but not trivial conclusion: With respect to any characteristic on which political systems differ, the greater the amount of variation or

[2] The subject of measurement and quantitative political analysis is vast, and the discussion here necessarily skims the surface. The topic is treated much more extensively in Edward R. Tufte, *Data Analysis for Politics and Policy* (Englewood Cliffs, N.J.: Prentice-Hall, Inc., 1974).

difference one's analysis can explain, the more useful or "powerful" the analysis is.

Yet the question remains whether "important" differences in political phenomena can be measured adequately. Clearly the utility of a science of politics depends heavily on the answer to this question. In arriving at an answer, the reader may wish to reflect on evidence contained in several of the earlier chapters in this book, particularly Chapters 6 and 7. Only a few years ago, attempts to measure the amount of "conflict" or "pluralism" in a country would have been regarded by most political scientists as absurd. They are still so regarded by many; but an increasing minority argue that even inadequate quantitative data are useful supplements to qualitative judgments that often rest upon highly impressionistic evidence.

Nonetheless, it would be premature to conclude that you will soon be able to make political choices on factual appraisals as solid as those in the natural sciences or engineering. There seems to be no satisfactory way to predict the rate at which factual knowledge required for political choices will increase. It is reasonable to conjecture that the flood of data now inundating us will in time be matched by an increase in verified hypotheses and theories. But the history of the natural sciences suggests that more data do not lead automatically to the discovery of nature's regularities.

Even under highly optimistic assumptions about the rate of increase in our factual knowledge, it seems quite clear that at present and in the near future a great many political choices are bound to be surrounded by a cloud of uncertainty. For in comparison with the natural sciences, medicine, or engineering, in which judgments about the value, moral quality, or goodness of different alternatives are ordinarily absent or relatively simple, in politics moral judgments are pervasive, powerful, and complex. The relative importance of a "fact," as we have seen, depends on one's standard of value.

Holistic Strategies. Since political choices are usually clouded by uncertainties, some students of decision-making have tried to develop strategies realistically adapted to situations of limited knowledge. Their approach is best seen as a reaction to strategies of perfect rationality, sometimes called *synoptic* or *holistic* approaches, that emphasize the desirability of a complete search for a rational answer before a choice is made. What is sometimes thought to be the ideal strategy of perfect rationality has been described as follows:

1. Faced with a given problem,
2. a rational man first clarifies his goals, values, or objectives, and then ranks or otherwise organizes them in his mind;
3. he then lists all important possible ways of—policies for—achieving his goals
4. and investigates all the important consequences that would follow from each of the alternative policies,

5. at which point he is in a position to compare consequences of each policy with goals
6. And so choose the policy with consequences most closely matching his goals[3]

This kind of strategy has great appeal—in the abstract. Yet in practice it is hardly more than a definition of perfect rationality; and perfect rationality has been unattainable, in politics as elsewhere. In practice, one is probably never in a position to acquire all the knowledge one needs for a completely rational decision on significant political questions.

Even if in practice a synoptic or holistic strategy is impossible to carry out completely, is it not, nevertheless, the ideal strategy? Even if we know we must fall short of perfect rationality, does not the synoptic strategy provide us with the model toward which we should aspire? Although the affirmative answer is tempting and plausible, in recent years critics have argued that the synoptic model is highly misleading. While it might provide a definition of perfect rationality, as a model for decision-making it is generally useless or even downright harmful.

Critics of the synoptic model[4] contend that in practice decision-makers rarely if ever go through the steps outlined above. Because of limitations in our knowledge, decisions are made—and *must* be made—in the midst of uncertainties. If we postponed decisions until we approached perfect rationality, we would never make a decision.

Strategies of Limited Rationality

In practice, you can cope with uncertainty in a number of useful ways. You can search for satisfactory rather than perfect solutions to problems. You can make a tentative decision and see what happens. You can take advantage of feedback, or information created by the initial decision itself.[5] As a result of feedback, you can change your goals, even highly important goals. You can usually assume, too, that the decision you will make is an endless series of steps, so that your errors can be corrected as you proceed. Thus you can frequently adopt an "incrementalist" strategy: Starting with an existing state of affairs about which a good deal is known, you can make small or incremental changes in the desired direction and then see what the next steps should be.

[3] Charles E. Lindblom, *The Policy-Making Process*, 2nd ed. (Englewood Cliffs, N.J.: Prentice-Hall, Inc., 1980).

[4] A leading critic of synoptic approaches to decision-making and an advocate of limited strategies is Lindblom, whose views will be found *ibid.*, particularly at pp. 14–27, and in D. Braybrooke and C. E. Lindblom, *A Strategy of Decision* (New York: Free Press, 1963). See also *The Intelligence of Democracy*. (New York: The Free Press, 1965). In *Politics and Markets* (New York: Basic Books, Inc., Publishers, 1977), though less enthusiastic about limited strategies, he is highly critical of the alleged rationality of comprehensive schemes of centralized planning. See esp. pp. 322–324.

[5] See Karl W. Deutsch, *The Nerves of Government* (New York: The Free Press, 1963), Chap. Eleven, "Government as a Process of Steering: The Concepts of Feedback, Goal, and Purpose," pp. 182–199.

You can go on making incremental changes indefinitely. A series of incremental changes can, in time, add up to a profound transformation: If you increase anything at the rate of 5 percent a year, you will double it in fourteen years.

Strategies that aim at perfect rationality are plausible and appealing, but they seem virtually impossible to execute. Strategies that aim at limited rationality seem somehow less "rational": yet in most situations limited strategies are all that you or anyone else will have for making decisions.

Experimental Strategies

Troubled by the high degree of uncertainty surrounding policy-making by governments, the comparatively low level of reliable knowledge on which decisions must be based, and palpable failures in policies produced both by holistic and by incremental strategies, some political analysts have begun to emphasize the possibility of reducing ignorance and uncertainty in policy-making by deliberate experimentation, or small-scale tryouts prior to the adoption of policies.

Obviously not all crucial decisions can be preceded by a small-scale tryout. Foreign policies, for example, hardly lend themselves to prior experimentation. The idea also creates images of inhumane experiments with powerless victims, such as prisoners who may be coerced into participating or ill-informed subjects whose "consent" is gained by manipulative persuasion.

Proponents of experimentalism in policy-making point out, however, that in practice, governments do make decisions on a variety of matters with wholly inadequate knowledge about the results to be expected. Not only are policies adopted that would be rejected if the results had been correctly foreseen; policies are also rejected that would have been adopted if the outcomes were better understood. Adopting or rejecting policy alternatives has favorable and harmful consequences for millions of people and costs billions of dollars in both private and public outlays. Thus policy decisions do in fact "experiment" with the welfare and happiness of people. But this experimentation is large scale, costly, and lacks all the criteria of a scientific experiment designed to produce reliable knowledge. Hence, often it would be feasible and much more reasonable, it is argued, to run small-scale, controlled, carefully studied tryouts in advance.[6]

Searching for Alternatives. None of these strategies can guarantee that it will lead to the discovery of the best available alternatives. As in the

[6] The Brookings Institution, Washington, D.C., has a Panel on Social Experimentation to "assess the usefulness of experiments as a way of increasing knowledge about the effects of domestic social policies and programs of the federal government." Studies include Edward M. Gramlich and Patricia P. Koshel, *Educational Performance Contracting: An Evaluation of an Experiment* (1975); Joseph A. Pechman and P. Michael Timpane, eds., *Work Incentives and Income Guarantees: The New Jersey Negative Income Tax Experiment* (1975); and Alice M. Rivlin and P. Michael Timpane, eds., *Planned Variation: Should We Give Up or Try Harder?* (1975).

arts, in science, in mathematics, or in the exploration of space, discovery requires an imaginative search.

There is, then, an indispensable need in political analysis for the informed imagination; for speculation, guided by knowledge, that transcends the received truths; for the design and contemplation of Utopias; for a willingness to think hard about unthinkable alternatives to all the too easily thinkable solutions. There is, in short, a need for a creative search inspired by the hunch that somewhere between the unattainable best and the kind of mediocrity so often attained in political matters there lies a universe of better alternatives—and worse ones, too—all waiting to be explored.

11

TO EXPLORE FURTHER

The reader who wishes to explore topics touched on in this book should consult the footnotes, for I have cited those references not so much to provide authority for what I have written as to indicate where the interested reader might go for further information.

An important source is *The Handbook of Political Science*, ed. Fred I. Greenstein and Nelson W. Polsby, 8 vols. (Reading, Mass.: Addison-Wesley Publishing Co., 1975). Although I have cited only a few of the *Handbook* articles in the footnotes, there are articles in the eight volumes that touch on practically every chapter in this book.

For the reader who may wish to go beyond the *Handbook* and the works cited in the footnotes, a few additional references may be helpful.

A great number of books and articles are directly relevant to the matters covered in Chapter 3, "Political Influence," and Chapter 4, "Forms of Influence." Nagel's book, cited in Chapter Three, footnote 6, contains a lengthy bibliography. A useful collection of articles will be found in Roderick Bell, David V. Edwards, and R. Harrison Wagner, *Political Power, A Reader in Theory and Research* (New York: The Free Press, 1969), which also has a good bibliography. For recent analyses with many citations to previous writings, see the 1981 book by Braam cited in Chapter 3, footnote 1; Dennis Wrong, *Power* (Harper & Row Publishers, Inc., 1979); and Nelson Polsby,

Community Power and Political Theory (New Haven: Yale University Press, 1980). For earlier work, see Andrew S. McFarland, *Power and Leadership in Pluralist Systems* (Stanford, Calif.: Stanford University Press, 1969); William A. Gamson, *Power and Discontent* (Homewood, Ill.: Dorsey Press, 1968); and my article "Power" in the *International Encyclopedia of the Social Sciences*, ed. David L. Sills (New York: Macmillan, Inc. and The Free Press, 1968).

A book critical of some of my own earlier formulations is Steven Lukes, *Power: A Radical View* (London: Macmillan, Inc., 1974). The topic discussed in Chapter Four is explored from a perspective somewhat different from my own by David V. J. Bell in *Power, Influence, and Authority* (New York: Oxford University Press, 1975).

Important contributions to our understanding of the similarities, differences, and development of political systems will be found in volume 3 of *The Handbook of Political Science.* See in particular Samuel P. Huntington and Jorge I. Dominguez, "Political Development," Juan J. Linz, "Totalitarian and Authoritarian Regimes," and Charles Tilly, "Revolutions and Collective Violence." A collection of essays on one-party systems is in Samuel P. Huntington and Clement H. Moore, *Authoritarian Politics in Modern Society* (New York: Basic Books, Inc., Publishers, 1970). A highly influential book on the nature of political development is Huntington's *Political Order in Changing Societies* (New Haven: Yale University Press, 1968). On the failure of democratic orders, see Juan J. Linz and Alfred Stepan, *The Breakdown of Democratic Regimes* (Baltimore: Johns Hopkins Press, 1978), 4 vols.

In addition to the work cited in footnote 5 in Chapter 8, Verba and Nie have contributed an article, "Political Participation," to volume 4 of the *Handbook*. The volume also contains Philip E. Converse, "Public Opinion and Voting Behavior." In volume 3, a particularly relevant article is David O. Sears, "Political Socialization."

Political Evaluation (Chapter 9) is the subject of voluminous and controversial literature. A good place to begin is with the works cited in the footnotes to that chapter. The book by Galston cited in footnote 13 provides brief, clear exposition on many writers from Galston's own critical perspective. See also J. Roland Pennock and John W. Chapman, *Nomos XXIII, Human Rights* (New York: New York University Press, 1981); their *Nomos VI, Justice* (New York: Lieber-Atherton, 1974); and the special issues of *Ethics*, on representation, Vol. 91, No. 3 (April, 1981) and on rights, Vol. 92, No. 1 (October, 1981). The journal *Ethics* has become an important center for discussions of issues of the kind described in Chapter 9.

The following list, though incomplete, includes some of the books published since about 1970 that illustrate the revival of Anglo-American political philosophy:

Carole Pateman, *Participation and Democratic Theory* (Cambridge: Cambridge University Press, 1970).

Robert Paul Wolff, *In Defense of Anarchism* (New York: Harper & Row Publishers, Inc., 1970, 1976).

C. B. Macpherson, *Democratic Theory: Essays in Retrieval* (Oxford: Clarendon Press, 1973).

Robert Nozick, *Anarchy, State and Utopia* (New York: Basic Books, Inc., Publishers, 1975).

Michael Walzer, *Just and Unjust Wars* (New York: Basic Books, Inc., Publishers, 1977).

Steven Lukes, *Essays in Social Theory* (London: Macmillan Press Ltd., 1977).

Charles Fried, *Right and Wrong* (Cambridge: Harvard University Press, 1977).

Ronald Dworkin, *Taking Rights Seriously* (Cambridge: Harvard University Press, 1978).

James Fishkin, *Tyranny and Legitimacy: A Critique of Political Theories* (Baltimore: Johns Hopkins, 1979); and *The Limits of Obligation* (New Haven: Yale University Press, 1980).

Bruce Ackerman, *Social Justice in the Liberal State* (New Haven: Yale University Press, 1980).

Douglas Rae, *Equalities* (Cambridge: Harvard University Press, 1981).

Chapter 10, "Choosing Policies: Strategies of Inquiry and Decision," is a fearfully brief treatment of a highly complex subject. The nature of scientific thought and the special characteristics of the social or human sciences are entire subjects in themselves. A brief description of Volume 6 of the *Handbook* is concerned with policies and policy-making. Other sources include Austin Ranney, ed., *Political Science and Public Policy* (Chicago: Markham, 1968), Richard I. Hofferbert, *The Study of Public Policy* (Indianapolis: The Bobbs Merrill Co., Inc., 1974), Ira Sharkansy and Donald Van Meter, *Policy and Politics in American Governments* (New York: McGraw-Hill Book Co., 1975) and William B. Gwyn and George C. Edwards, III, eds., *Perspectives on Policy Making* (New Orleans: Tulane Univ., 1975).

INDEX